# A
# MISSING
# P·E·A·C·E

### VIETNAM:
### FINALLY HEALING
### THE PAIN

# Robert Seiple

*with Gregg Lewis*

INTERVARSITY PRESS
DOWNERS GROVE, ILLINOIS 60515

©1992 by Robert Seiple

InterVarsity Press is the book-publishing division of InterVarsity Christian Fellowship, a student movement active on campus at hundreds of universities, colleges and schools of nursing in the United States of America, and a member movement of the International Fellowship of Evangelical Students. For information about local and regional activities, write Public Relations Dept., InterVarsity Christian Fellowship, 6400 Schroeder Rd., P.O. Box 7895, Madison, WI 53707-7895.

All Scripture quotations, unless otherwise indicated, are from the HOLY BIBLE, NEW INTERNATIONAL VERSION. Copyright © 1973, 1978, 1984 International Bible Society. Used by permission of Zondervan Publishing House. All rights reserved.

ISBN 0-8308-1294-6

Printed in the United States of America ∞

Library of Congress Cataloging-in-Publication Data
Seiple, Robert A., 1942-
    A missing peace: Vietnam: Finally healing the pain/Robert
Seiple with Gregg Lewis.
      p.    cm.
    "Saltshaker books"—P.
    ISBN 0-8308-1294-6
    1. Vietnamese Conflict, 1961-1975.  2. Vietnam—Description and
travel—1975-    3. Vietnam—Relations—United States.  4. United
States—Relations—Vietnam.    I. Lewis, Gregg A.    II. Title.
DS557.7.S45    1991
959.704'3—dc20

              91-23242
              CIP

| 15 | 14 | 13 | 12 | 11 | 10 | 9 | 8 | 7 | 6 | 5 | 4 | 3 | 2 | 1 |
|----|----|----|----|----|----|----|----|----|----|----|----|----|----|----|
| 03 | 02 | 01 | 00 | 99 | 98 | 97 | 96 | 95 | 94 | 93 | 92 | | | |

# Prolog

I could feel the old Soviet-built TU-34 strain as it lumbered down the runway, using up most of the 12,000 feet of concrete before lifting ponderously into the air. The overbooked flight carried primarily high-ranking Vietnamese military personnel and a group of Cubans, six of whom had to stand in the aisle at the back of the plane for the entire trip—takeoff and landing included.

As if the crowded cabin wasn't uncomfortable enough, the plane's inoperative air conditioning system and the ninety-five-degree tropical heat combined to create a flying sauna. Having noted the frayed radial fibers showing through the plane's tread-bare tires as we boarded, I tried not to wonder about the working condition of the other, more vital parts of this aircraft.

Yet my mind refused to dwell on my discomfort or my uneasiness. My thoughts churned in a muddle of mixed emotions and memories.

For the better part of two decades, should anyone have asked me, "If you could visit any country in the world, where would you go?" I'd have answered immediately, "Vietnam!" Now here I was, in April 1988, in a Vietnam Airlines plane climbing into the clouds above Ho Chi Minh City (once Saigon) and banking north toward Hanoi.

We flew high above DaNang, but I could still make out some parts of the coastal city where I'd been stationed for thirteen months in the late sixties as a U.S. Marine bombardier/navigator in an A-6 attack jet. Every turn toward Hanoi, or "Bull's-eye" as we called it during the war, reminded me of target headings, coast-in points, and SAM batteries. I even recognized the familiar shape of an island thousands of feet below—a landmark I'd used numerous times to update my computerized navigational equipment and make sure our nighttime bombing runs were right on course.

I had no instruments to read this time. No settings to adjust. Nothing to focus my thoughts on except a sudden sense of nostalgia and a flood of twenty-year-old memories.

I've spent a lifetime planning and pursuing goals—professional and personal. I've lived looking forward, with seldom a glance in life's rearview mirror. Vietnam is the exception. At odd moments my memory tape will still flash back to some scene, some incident, some person I knew during the war.

Thirteen months "in country" etched the sights and sounds and smells of Vietnam deep in my memory—a repository of images which touched the very core of my being and yet always remained surprisingly close to the surface of my consciousness.

Over the years, I've come to the gradual realization that my Vietnam experience shaped my life and my being as nothing else could have done. It was here, in and over the jungles of Vietnam, that I was forced to face the meaning of life as well as the reality of death. It was here that I first wrestled with the real issues of truth and morality. It was here, over Vietnam, that I—like an entire generation of Americans—lost my innocence and finally grew up.

I'd longed to return—but not in some vain quest to recapture my lost youth. Not in any way wishing to relive the terrible, adrenalin-laced adventure of war. More like an old grad returning to his alma mater, I wanted to see once again the place that loomed so large in my personal history.

Looking down at the familiar jagged coastline where the varied, verdant greens of the triple-canopied jungle met the beautiful blues of the China Sea, it was easy to be mesmerized by my memories. But one look around the cabin of that ancient commercial airliner was enough to remind me that this flight to Hanoi was taking place in 1988 not 1968. So much had changed. So much was different this time.

\*　\*　\*　\*

The first time I'd come to Vietnam, I'd kissed my pregnant wife goodbye as she stood crying on a rainy runway in America's heartland; our oldest son had been born in my absence three months later. This time Margaret Ann accompanied me, along with our youngest son, twelve-year-old Jesse.

The last time I'd flown this way I'd been hunched over a radar screen, trying to ignore the flak exploding around my plane, listening for the dreaded warning signal that a surface-to-air missile had locked on us, observing total radio silence, and hoping the enemy wouldn't know exactly where we were or guess where we were going until we dropped our bombs on target and hightailed it for the coast. This time I flew toward Hanoi not as an enemy airman but as the invited guest of the Vietnamese government, to be met not by tracers spewing across the dark night sky but by officials of the Communist regime in Hanoi.

In 1967-68, as a captain in the Marine Corps, I did what I was trained to do and carried out my duty to my country. Now, in 1988, I was returning as president of World Vision.

During my first time in Vietnam I'd dropped more than 1700 tons of explosives on the country. This time I came bringing materials and equipment to make artificial limbs for the 60,000 Vietnamese people disabled by more than a generation of war. The last time I'd flown toward Hanoi my flight was an act of war. Twenty years later I was returning in an act of friendship, Christian compassion and reconciliation. This time I wanted to make things better for suffering

Vietnamese people, to finally do some good in a place where my previous efforts, and those of my country, had done so little good.

This visit, one of my first overseas trips as president of World Vision, seemed like a new beginning to me. So much was different this time. So much had changed—for me.

Yet for the Vietnamese people much remained the same. The fast-growing jungle, once ravaged by napalm and bombs, had mercifully covered some scars of war. The countryside appeared green and fertile again. But there was very little industry. No smokestacks, just tiny villages bisected by a few dirt roads. In twenty years, very little had changed.

Countless bomb craters could be seen from the air on our approach into Hanoi—lasting reminders of the B-52 raids Richard Nixon had ordered sixteen years before. Two days in Ho Chi Minh City (formerly Saigon, capital of the South) before flying to Hanoi had told much the same story of disrepair and decline—evident from the moment we landed at the capital's Tan Son Nhut airport.

Ours was the only operable plane in sight the day we landed at Tan Son Nhut—once one of the busiest airports in the world. Rusting hulks of C-47s and C-130s littered the perimeter of the field. The old rivetments were empty except for a few burned-out helicopters. And the ride into Ho Chi Minh City from the airport gave us our first glimpse of the time warp we were to see throughout Vietnam: old cars (nothing newer than the mid-seventies), trucks older than that, and buildings even older—all in desperate need of repair.

You couldn't spend any time at all in Vietnam in 1988 without realizing that the impact of the war continues still, more than a quarter-century after America got involved. You sense it when you look at the Vietnamese landscape. But you *know* it when you look into the faces of those affected by the war—the victims on both sides of the Pacific.

\* \* \* \*

Here is yet another difference between my first Vietnam experience and my second. Dropping bombs from an airplane flying five hundred miles an hour I could see only geography—jungle, mountains, rivers, roads—and blips on my radar screen indicating mechanical targets such as trucks and artillery batteries. A bombardier/navigator can't see any faces. But as president of World Vision, looking for ways to help people in need, I must see the faces. And that makes for a very different experience. By the time I took that 1988 plane flight into Hanoi, I'd already seen some of those faces. Others I would encounter in Hanoi or on subsequent trips to Vietnam.

There was the beautifully innocent face of a three-year-old girl suffering from polio because her country continues to spend forty-five per cent of its GNP on its military while failing to provide the most rudimentary health care and vaccinations to its children. Then there was the mutilated face of a twenty-year-old boy who stepped on a land mine buried and forgotten before he was even born.

There's the sad face of an Amerasian girl, the daughter of an American soldier and a Vietnamese woman, who tries to meet every foreign flight landing at Tan Son Nhut, in hopes that she'll be there when the father she doesn't remember returns for her. There are also the determined faces of Vietnamese Christians, many of whom spent the better part of a decade in re-education camps, who continue to try to worship and live out their faith in a country that still routinely restricts and persecutes pastors and religious leaders.

On this side of the ocean there are others. The wary faces of thousands of Vietnam vets who have tried to flee both civilization and their own memories of the war to live among the forests and mountains of the American Northwest. The hopeful faces of Vietnam immigrants who have made a new home here without forgetting their original homeland. The grown-up faces of young men and women who have lived a lifetime wondering about MIA fathers they can recall only when prompted by faded photographs and flickering images in old home movies. And the angry, despairing faces in veterans' hospitals—men still suffering the inescapable effects of debilitating war wounds or the ravages of Agent Orange.

On both sides of the Pacific I've seen the hardened faces of government officials who still see the same issues, still articulate the old arguments they've used for a generation. In all these faces, belonging to people we'll meet in more detail later in this book, I see undeniable evidence that *the Vietnam war is indeed a war without closure.*

\* \* \* \*

But there are other faces as well—faces of people who have challenged me to think about my own response, taught me valuable lessons and given me hope for the healing of the wounds caused by this conflict and any conflict. And we'll meet some of these people in the pages of this book. The bureaucratic Vietnamese commander I butted heads with when I demanded to visit my old barracks on a restricted DaNang military base. My own twelve-year-old son, Jesse, whose sense of diplomacy proved more effective than the power of an American president. A generous Vietnamese cyclo driver who convicted me with a question we all must wrestle with. And a blind, retarded Vietnamese boy who sang me a song so powerful I'll never ever forget it.

In some ways this is a very personal book. It is one man's accounting of his Vietnam experience and the faces he encountered there—during the war and now more recently. Just as my war experience helped shape me into the person I am today, my recent Vietnam experiences are teaching me more about the kind of person I want to be for the rest of my life.

But this is more than a book about my personal pilgrimage, and it's more than a book about Vietnam.

There are many lessons still to learn from Vietnam. Not just for the millions of us whose lives were touched by the war. Not just for a nation that wants to avoid future mistakes, in battle and after the shooting stops.

There are lessons for anyone who has experienced conflict—on any level—and is now missing that satisfying, positive peace that can and should be ours.

# Part I
## Loss of
## Innocence

# 1
# Here Comes the Marine!

October 1967. The final goodbye.

A cold evening rain drizzled from the dreary gray clouds hanging low over the Quad Cities Airport in Moline, Illinois, as I embraced my sobbing wife and kissed her goodbye. Tears mixed with rain streamed down her face as I finally turned, hurried across the wet tarmac and mounted the steps of the waiting plane.

Next stop California, where I was to report to Norton Air Force Base for a military charter flight to Okinawa. Then on to Vietnam for a thirteen-month tour of duty.

When I'd stowed my gear and taken my seat, I pressed my face to the window and looked for Margaret Ann. There she was at the gate—soaked with rain, already bulging with six months of pregnancy, crying and waving pathetically at the plane's darkened cabin windows in hopes that I could still see her. I did—but I had to quickly turn away to deal with my own tears.

I hadn't expected this to be so tough. I'd already said farewells to my parents and friends back east before bringing Margaret Ann to her folks' home in Iowa. That New Jersey leave-taking from my family had proved far easier than anticipated—not at all the emotional trauma I'd experienced when I'd left for basic training nearly two years before.

Margaret Ann and I had talked about this parting day since the beginning and before. We'd been married under crossed swords in a military wedding during my flight training in Pensacola, Florida. Margaret Ann took me as her lawfully wedded husband knowing I didn't bring a million-dollar dowry or even twenty camels. What she got when she said yes was a declaration of my eternal love, along with the almost certain prospect that I would be leaving her for thirteen long months sometime during the first three years of marriage.

I took her willingness to marry me under these circumstances as a true measure of her love.

When, less than a year into our marriage, she told me she wanted to be pregnant before I left for Vietnam, part of me wanted to protest the idea. I realized that if something happened to me in Vietnam, her life would be much easier if she had only herself to worry about. But Margaret Ann was so sure; she said she wanted a tangible reminder of our love.

Standing there in the rain, six months pregnant, she looked extremely tangible. I took that as yet another measure of her love for me—a love that gave me a wonderfully heartening sense of hope and strength at that moment of parting while at the same time stirring up within my soul a sense of despair more terrible than anything I'd known in my twenty-three years of life.

But then, strong emotion hadn't played a big part in my growing-up years in a small, rural New Jersey village nearly as idyllic as its name: Harmony. We majored in stability; my parents gave their six kids a strong sense of security and we were a supportive family. Born into the solid-rock fundamentalist faith of my parents, I laughingly tell people I think I was saved in the fifth month of my mother's pregnancy and during the sixth month became a Republican. Eventually I reached the point where I consciously affirmed my parents' faith as my own, but it was a gradual, natural process rather than a once-and-for-all decision I can point to at a certain time and place.

Harmony was a one-stop-sign town—an almost perfect place for a kid to grow up. My big brother Bill and I divided the year into three seasons—football, basketball and baseball—and played them all with our friends. We earned spending money working on the same Delaware Valley farms where we also hunted and fished in season.

I found it easy to be a Christian in that environment where all the issues seemed as black and white as the Holstein cows grazing on our green New Jersey hillsides. We experienced a minimum of testing. I had few conflicts or cares. And if there were ever any questions or doubts we could look up the answers in the Scofield Bible.

Like a lot of kids with very talented and capable older siblings, I grew up with the compelling psychological need to live up to the example of my big brother and with the underlying subconscious fear that maybe I'd never be good enough to escape his shadow. So competition became a way of life that permeated every area of my adolescent experience—not just sports, but school, work, church, even my social life.

Something within me embraced the role of underdog. Looking back, I can see it was primarily the psychological undergirding of my solid family upbringing and the strong foundational values of my parents that gave me the confidence to look self-doubt in the face and accept most any challenge. I was always ready to climb out on a limb, then fight like crazy to hang on and avoid that dreaded, ever-present prospect of failure.

My undergraduate years at Brown University provided me with a new challenge—a challenge to my faith. I'd never known an agnostic, let alone a self-declared atheist before. The idea that someone might question the basis of my personal spiritual convictions, or actually take offense at my religious beliefs, came as a complete surprise. However, that big bucket of ice-cold intellectualism dumped on my spiritual and theological naiveté failed to douse the flame of my personal faith.

I'm afraid I rather relished the role of spiritual underdog, adamantly defending my beliefs at every opportunity—during class and in my dorm. In retrospect, I have to admit I often tried to share my spiritual convictions with all the tact and delicacy of a ten-pound sledgehammer. Yet perhaps the greatest of the many benefits garnered from my wonderful education at Brown was that I was forced for the first time to honestly examine and clearly articulate my Christian faith.

I graduated with an excellent academic preparation for life and no sense of purpose or direction for my life. Since the only real experience I'd had through sixteen years of school was in education, it seemed the natural thing to do with a literature degree would be to teach. So by the time I walked across the platform to receive my college diploma, plans were already in motion to return to Brown that next fall to begin a masters program in literature with the thought of an eventual academic career.

**Summer Adventure**
But first, this country boy from New Jersey decided to do what so many of his peers were doing in the summer of 1965. I loaded up a backpack and sailed off to see the world—or at least as much of

Europe as I could cover in ten weeks. My college roommate and I took a ship to France, caught a train to Germany where we bought a Volkswagen Beetle and then wandered all over Europe—exploring and sightseeing.

Yet the most life-impacting experience of the entire trip took place not in Europe, but on the way home, aboard an old World War 2-vintage tanker that had been refitted and converted into a virtual cattle-boat crammed with 1500 college students. It was there that I met Margaret Ann. Her assigned seat during meals was only four tables away from mine.

I noticed her right away because she was so attractive. But I also noticed a large engagement ring on her finger. I'm not sure which of those factors best explains why it took me five days to work up the nerve to introduce myself.

I immediately learned she was a solid Midwesterner, with an independent mind and a readiness to put me in my place. She laughed at my jokes, but seemed to take some delight in puncturing my ego. Once we'd met, the fact that she was engaged did nothing to squelch my interest; if anything it heightened the competitive challenge and my desire to get to know this intriguing young lady in the four days we had left. By the time we sailed past the Statue of Liberty and docked in New York, I knew I wanted to pursue a relationship. When we disembarked and said goodbye, I promised to see her again as soon as possible. She acted as if she didn't believe me. But I vowed not to let her get away.

We corresponded over the next three months as I took a full-time job in the Brown admissions office. I wasn't the most faithful letter writer. In fact, Margaret Ann scolded me when I didn't write long or good letters. Once, after writing her a very brief missive, I got a "Why bother?" note in return.

Her feistiness made her all the more attractive. I decided I would visit her on one of my admissions trips to the Midwest. I had to be in Minneapolis; she was working in Iowa; we got together for one day before I needed to return to Providence. That night she broke off her engagement and I flew east a happier young man. In the weeks that followed our own long-distance relationship continued to develop and grow.

### The Draft Board Calls

But another thread was being simultaneously woven into my life story that fall of 1965. I received a letter from my local draft board informing me that the build-up of American forces in Vietnam raised the very real prospect that I might soon be drafted. While this development prompted me to put off the start of my planned Master of Arts in Teaching program, I can't say this news seemed either surprising or particularly distressing.

Growing up where I did during the forties and fifties, patriotism naturally was an integral part of my identity. I not only held a deep and genuine love for my country, I felt a sense of obligation for what being an American meant to me personally. I'd heard John F. Kennedy's challenge to "ask not what your country can do for you . . ." I had experienced a wonderful upbringing, received a college scholarship and graduated debt-free with an Ivy League education. And so far my country had asked nothing from me in return.

The previous generation had fought World War 2 and Korea. Now, Vietnam was my generation's war. Between two and three million of my peers were already in uniform. I couldn't help feeling a compelling sense of duty and obligation.

If I was going to get called eventually, why wait? Why not embrace the challenge? And if it's challenge I'm looking for, why not the Marines? The few, the proud.

I called my brother, who was teaching school at the time, to inform him of my decision. "I'm gonna join the Marines."

"Good!" he told me. "I'll go with you."

## Basic Training

Neither of us will ever forget the cold January morning when we left home together for our basic OCS training down in Quantico, Virginia. Mom fixed us breakfast, and then, as we ate, she insisted on reading from her Bible—Psalm 91:

He who dwells in the shelter of the Most High will rest in the shadow of the Almighty.

I will say of the LORD, "He is my refuge and my fortress, my God, in whom I trust."

Surely he will save you from the fowler's snare and from the deadly pestilence.

He will cover you with his feathers, and under his wings you will find refuge; his faithfulness will be your shield and rampart.

You will not fear the terror of night, nor the arrow that flies by day . . .

I caught my brother's eye and wondered if his breakfast had suddenly become as tasteless as mine.

. . . nor the pestilence that stalks in the darkness, nor the plague that destroys at midday.

A thousand may fall at your side, ten thousand at your right hand, but it will not come near you.

Mom's voice, which had grown shakier with each verse, finally cracked. But she tried to read on.

For he will command his angels concerning you to guard you in all your ways; they will lift you up. . . .

She finally broke down completely, dissolving into tears. And it was the wrenching memory of that scene that loomed over Bill and me the entire drive to Virginia—what seemed like the longest trip of my life.

A black cloud of depression hung over me for days. That, plus the unprecedented experience of having a drill sergeant rouse me from sleep at 5:30 A.M. by beating on a garbage can with a baseball bat only to scream unreasonable orders and call me unprintable names, quickly convinced me that joining the U.S. Marines was the biggest mistake I'd ever made in my life. Worse was the horrible realization that this one stupid decision was going to cost four years of my life and there wasn't a single thing I could do to change it.

But as my depression and the initial shock of boot camp wore off, I began to focus on the challenge and competition. I discovered an almost perverse pleasure in the military discipline and even in the precision required for marching. I scored well enough in my Officer's Training School to choose where I'd go next; I chose flight school.

Margaret Ann came to graduation ceremonies to see me commissioned as a second lieutenant in the U.S. Marines. Then she went home with me to New Jersey for a couple days before I went with her to Iowa and met her family before I headed off to Florida for my flight training.

In May, just a few weeks later, during my weekend break between pre-flight and sea survival schools, Margaret Ann came to Pensacola and we were married in a small military ceremony attended by a total of thirty-five people. It certainly wasn't a big wedding with a lot of fanfare; but for the record, I'd have gotten married with less.

By the time we were married I'd known Margaret Ann for about nine months. We'd corresponded regularly during that time, but we'd spent a grand total of only eleven or twelve days in each other's company. Although I hesitate to recommend our courtship experience to others, I believe now, a quarter-century later, just what I believed then: getting married was the absolute right thing to do and ours was a marriage made and blessed in heaven.

While it certainly wasn't a picnic bouncing around the country to various training assignments, our newlywed life remained a romantic adventure. I'd never been happier.

Vision tests disqualified me from becoming a pilot, so I had a choice between training to be a radar-intercept officer in an F-4 or a bombardier/navigator in an A-6. The built-in computers, multiple radar, night-vision capability and all the electronic countermeasures of the A-6 seemed like the bigger challenge.

But before my training ended I regularly regretted my flight-school decision. The trainers we flew in had a built-in Dutch roll in the rear of the plane which created such a nauseatingly constant rolling motion that I threw up on most of my training flights. Which explained why I graduated from fighter-intercept school thinner than at any other point in my adult life.

### Departure

I received my orders for Vietnam in the spring of 1967—to arrive in country and begin my tour in October. I remember my sense of excitement as I rushed back to the apartment that day to tell Margaret Ann even though I knew she couldn't really understand or share my anticipation.

I couldn't adequately articulate my own feelings. It wasn't that I thought going off to war would be some wonderful adventure. And it certainly wasn't that I looked forward to leaving my new wife for thirteen months.

I saw it as my duty. I wanted to do my duty because it was what I'd been trained for. And to some degree, I have to admit, I wanted to go because I sensed the experience would provide me with the greatest challenge of my life. Maybe the ultimate challenge.

Margaret Ann and I talked out our plans at length. She'd live with her folks in Iowa. She'd have the baby there and her parents would help her survive those first few months of single parenthood.

I would have a week of R & R in Hawaii halfway through my tour. But at that point the baby would be three or four months old and very demanding. The trip from Iowa would be rough and expensive; so we'd save our money and wait instead for a nice long leave at the end of the entire tour. We'd write every day, she'd send me pictures of the baby, and we'd make it. We had it all planned out.

It had all seemed so doable when we'd talked through the details. Not until I was sitting in the plane on that Illinois runway, experiencing the same horrible anguish inside me that I saw on Margaret Ann's face as she waved from the gate, did I finally begin to imagine how long thirteen months would be.

Within a week I would change our plans and begin planning my week of R & R in Hawaii with the woman I loved and the baby who would one day call me dad. Within a month I would come to believe I had very little chance of surviving thirteen months of combat. But it would take decades for me to begin to understand how Vietnam— the people and the experiences I would face there—would ultimately change my life.

# 2
# Introduction
# to
# Danger

★

I arrived in DaNang with a planeload of military personnel aboard a Continental Airlines flight from Okinawa. Pretty American flight attendants wearing short-skirted western outfits complete with cowboy hats bid us good-bye at the cabin door—a final flash of almost surrealistic Americana as we stepped out of the plane into the world and war.

My brother, who'd been commissioned as an infantry officer and had shipped out to Vietnam soon after our OCS training, met me in DaNang. Bill's thirteen-month tour had actually ended a few days earlier, but he'd opted to wait to head home so he could personally welcome me to Vietnam.

Our reunion only lasted a few hours. And as much as I appreciated his caring enough to meet me, the experience was probably more sobering than encouraging. Because the brother I'd known growing up was undeniably different now.

It wasn't so much what Bill said. In fact, I don't even remember what we talked about. The difference was in the way he looked—his total bearing. He'd always been tougher than I was, which was one reason I had let him do so much of my fighting for me when we were kids. But there was a disconcerting aura of hardness about him now—a sense of worldliness I'd never seen in him before.

Time and tropical conditions had faded his fatigues and well-worn jungle boots to a nondescript brown. The .45 pistol on his belt seemed almost a permanent part of him. He looked to me like someone who'd been to hell and back. Yet everything about him—from the confidence with which he walked to the wariness in his eyes to the Purple Heart he'd earned—marked him as a survivor.

Unsettling as that reunion was for me, I think it scared Bill even more. There before him stood his little brother, greener than grass, greener even than the new starched fatigues I wore, knowing nothing of what I'd face in the coming thirteen months. To his eyes, I looked so pathetic and unprepared that he feared for my survival.

I didn't realize the depth of his fears right then. I began to understand only when my mom wrote to tell me about Bill's homecoming. He'd been asked to share, in his first service back in our home church, about his experience overseas. He'd stood and talked briefly, expressing his gratitude for the sense of God's grace and protection he had experienced in Vietnam. In closing he reminded our hometown congregation that I was just now beginning my tour in Vietnam. Then he started to ask them to please remember to pray for me. At that point, my mother wrote, he'd gotten so choked up he couldn't say any more.

Such public displays of emotion were not a Seiple trait. So reading Mom's letter about Bill's uncharacteristic behavior hit me hard. I knew then how much the war had changed my brother. And I knew I could only imagine the intensity of what he'd faced, what I was going to experience myself in the coming months.

## In War, People Die

Someone once said the reason men go to war is that the women are watching. And even now in a day when women soldiers routinely draw combat duty, I suspect there's still a lot of truth to that statement—a lot of jingoistic machismo. It probably accounts at least partly for my own youthfully naive feelings about "my duty, my country, my generation, my war." Certainly wanting to prove myself factored into my choice of the Marines and then flight school, as well as my excitement over my orders to Vietnam.

But it wasn't long before reality punctured that balloon.

I lost two roommates the first month I was in DaNang. I'd gone through training with Steve. So his was a familiar face when I arrived a few weeks after he did. I was pleased to be assigned as his roommate, but we never had time to renew our friendship because his plane was shot down during my first week in country, while on an ill-conceived bombing mission to a bridge just outside Hanoi.

Bob was a career Marine and also a good friend from training school. We'd spent a lot of time together fishing in central Florida whenever we could get away from the base. A couple weeks after Steve went down, Bob disappeared on a night mission over Haiphong while flying as bombardier/navigator for our squad's commanding officer.

Of the fifteen air crews assigned to our squadron, we had lost two crews and two planes in just three weeks. The arithmetic didn't look good. The hard numbers said none of us were going to make it, and odds like that took any sense of adventure out of war in a hurry.

The naive notion of proving myself quickly gave way to a more realistic sensation: fear. I began to think that if I could go home honorably any way short of shooting myself in the foot, I'd gladly do it! I also began to seriously consider the question: *How am I possibly going to survive for thirteen months?*

Everyone asked himself that same question. But different people answered it differently.

You could buy hard liquor for a quarter a drink at the base officer's club, which meant you could get drunk for fifty cents. With temptation that handy and cheap, a few guys tried to handle the pressure by living and sometimes even flying on the edge between sober and drunk.

Another, less dangerous coping strategy was sleep. And a lot of fliers perfected this skill to a fine art, figuring if you could manage to sleep twelve hours a day, every day, thirteen months would seem only half as long. Not a bad plan.

Some fliers, no one ever knew how many, tried to survive by weaseling out of the toughest assignments or by simply going through the motions. I knew officers who would drop by the operations center early in the day to see what their mission was to be that night. If they pulled a "deep-North" assignment rather than an easier flight over South Vietnam, they'd head to the briefing room to check out the target folder for any information on the enemy armaments and defenses they could expect to encounter. Some time after that, if the flight looked pretty dangerous, they would wander over to sick bay complaining of sniffles and get a "down chit" that excused them from flying that night because of a head cold. This was not the usual thing; most of the guys performed their duty as well as they could despite the constant, gnawing fear. But it happened. And I could understand it.

Then there was the standard joke about pilots flying a thousand feet higher for every month they'd been in country. This meant a new guy would fly by the book, fast and low, just a few hundred feet off the ground. By the second month he'd be closer to two thousand feet, the next month three thousand, until the end of his tour when he'd be perfectly content to drop his payload from a couple miles up, well out of range of any small-arms ground fire.

While that was of course an exaggeration, there was a very natural tendency to grow more cautious and take fewer risks as you became more experienced. Maybe that was because the more times you dropped your load of bombs on a suspected "enemy truck park" or a "strategic supply route," only to level another few acres of empty jungle or leave a few craters in a deserted cow path, the less crucial any one mission seemed. And if you seriously pondered the question "Is tonight's mission a target worth dying for?" the honest answer nearly always seemed to be "No!"

Which was why some crews assigned targets deep over North Vietnam would suddenly encounter a mysterious sort of "mechanical problem" that would force them to abort the mission and turn back. Or they might not even try to reach the target, opting to drop their bombs at sea without ever entering enemy air space.

Most flights were single-plane missions, so no one besides the pilot and bombardier/navigator was there to know where a plane actually went when it dropped down beneath radar cover. The pilot was supposed to radio the code "Feet dry" when he passed over the coast into enemy territory, and then observe strict radio silence until he dropped his bombs, flew safely back to the coast and declared "Feet wet!" But there was nothing except two men's sense of conscience and duty to keep them from simply dumping their bombs into the ocean without risking hostile fire, then flying low circles for an appropriate amount of time before calling "Feet wet!" and heading back to base acting as if they'd done their job.

A few guys, probably very few, did that. I suppose they thought that was the only way to survive; survival instinct could be an incredibly powerful drive.

### Staying Alive

My own primary coping mechanism was to fly.

I got assigned duty as scheduling officer early in my tour. That meant every other day I helped determine the mission assignments and could slot myself for a flight whenever possible. The pilot I flew with most of the time had the same duty on the alternate days. So we easily arranged to fly together and often. I tried not to log the most flights during a given month—because the busiest pilot and bombardier automatically drew lighter duty the following month. Most months I managed to rank second on the list of aviators. Since no one seemed to look below the very top of the list, I ended up flying a lot of missions month after month—an average of almost one mission per day for most of my tour.

My total of three hundred flights earned me a total of twenty-eight Air Medals, a Vietnam Campaign Medal with five battle stars, the Navy Commendation award and the Distinguished Flying Cross. But it wasn't any quest for honors that motivated me. Neither did I have any strong drive to fight. Flying was simply the best way I knew to cope with the unavoidable pressures of combat.

The more missions I flew, the more time I spent flying and preparing to fly, the faster the days and weeks seemed to pass. Doing what I'd been trained for, going through all the now familiar routines, actually reduced that constant undertone of tension and fear. It certainly seemed to beat the alternatives of inactivity, waiting and worry.

Being in the air, doing my job, was the only way for me to feel a sense of control in an otherwise uncontrollable environment. I realize there was a degree of absurdity in this attitude because a bombardier/navigator in an A-6 aircraft was never truly in control. But at least I had *chosen* to be there.

The pilot did the actual flying while I sat next to him in the cockpit, hunched over my radar screens, plotting and rechecking our course, watching and feeding the various on-board computers. I would set the ballistics and tell him when "the pickle was hot" and the bombs were ready to drop. But the computer actually dropped the bombs when the pilot maneuvered the plane into position.

If something happened to him, I had neither the training nor the instruments on my side of the cockpit to land the plane. About the only time I pulled my head out of my radar-screen hood was when the flashing lights on the control panel and the terrifying warble in my headphones signalled the launch of a SAM, a surface-to-air missile. At that point two pairs of eyes were needed to search the black sky outside the cockpit for the white-hot trail of a missile zeroing in on us. The only sure way to escape a radar-controlled SAM was to spot it, turn the nose toward it, and play what amounted to a very deadly game of chicken—waiting until the last possible second and then throwing the plane into such a sharp turn that the missile (traveling two to three thousand miles per hour) couldn't change course fast enough and would hurtle harmlessly past.

But even then, when it came to evading enemy fire, the reflexes that mattered, the split-second decisions that made the difference between life and death, were the pilot's. While we worked together as a team and he needed me to complete any mission, my life was always completely in his hands.

And yet, as irrational as it seems, flying gave me the only real sense of control I felt in Vietnam. Perhaps it was merely the illusion of control, but doing something, even if it was just my duty, made me feel as if I had some say in the matter of my own survival.

The truth was, survival was a constant, underlying consideration at all times—even when we weren't flying. You could never afford to let down your guard because there wasn't much "friendly territory" anywhere in Vietnam. I never felt safe the few times I ventured into the city of DaNang. I think I went over to China Beach once. For the most part I was content to spend my ground time within the barricaded, barbed-wire confines of our DaNang air base. Even then many hours were spent on survival tasks—like adding extra layers of green nylon sandbags to the bunkers we used during mortar attacks.

Not even the base could be considered a safe haven, as we were reminded on many a night when the Vietcong would sneak in close enough to lob in mortar or small-rocket fire. The weapons were so notoriously inaccurate, the chances of doing much damage or hitting a plane so slim, that these Vietcong gunners had to be courageous or crazy to try it and very lucky to survive it. Although incoming fire would send everyone bolting for cover and bring any landing or launch operations to an immediate halt, the disruption was only temporary. The typical response to any such fire was to spot the origin of attack and call in a C-47 with a Gatling gun to fly over the area in a prescribed pattern, unleashing an almost solid curtain of tracers from the night sky that could riddle a patch of jungle with a bullet every three inches.

**Attack!**

However, the enemy could get lucky. We'd just returned from a mission one night, had refueled the planes and were getting ready to park them between the protective rivetments when the Vietcong launched a multiple missile attack. I leaped from my plane and sprinted toward my bunker. I heard the incoming mortar rounds landing closer and closer behind me as if they were tracking me across the runway. Any second I expected to feel chunks of hot metal slash into my body.

A final few steps and I threw myself at the bunker as yet another rocket exploded behind me. In the dark and desperation I couldn't find the shelter's door. So I lay there, still outside but plastered atop the bunker roof until the flash of the next explosion gave me light enough to spot the door and dive under cover.

Twenty or more rockets landed harmlessly before the explosions stopped. Then we waited and listened to ninety seconds of silence before a final, lone rocket came screaming in. Peering out from my bunker I saw it score a direct hit on one of our fully gassed, fully armed jets. The incredible explosion of first the plane, then the bombs, set off other explosions. The resulting fireball roared from one plane to another, creating fireworks of epic proportions as fuel tanks and bombs exploded one after another and in turn triggered cockpit charges which sent ejection seats blasting into the air above the flames.

All the crews raced out onto the field to haul bombs and other planes away from the growing inferno. But before it was over we'd lost a total of five planes as well as one of our hangars—a convincing reminder that we were never completely safe.

# 3
# Will I
# Live to Go
# Home?

One of the most common coping mechanisms for dealing with the constant danger and fear during war is to try to detach yourself from your emotions and sometimes even from the terrible reality of the events taking place around you. Looking back, I marvel at how quickly I learned to do this—to deaden my natural reactions.

## Easy Denial

I'd drawn the assignment of All-Night Operations Officer the night I lost my second roommate, just three weeks into my tour. All-night duty basically meant that from midnight to six A.M. I was responsible for keeping track of the planes ready to be launched and the flights in progress or already returned. In brief, I was supposed to answer the phones and keep an eye on all the squad's flight operations until someone relieved me in the morning—a very dull job most nights.

I was sitting at the desk in the early morning hours, reading a book, when I took the call from central control reporting Bob's flight as "overdue." That was simply a military euphemism meaning a plane had been gone for longer than it had fuel for and there was no longer any chance that it would return.

I acknowledged the information, hung up the phone, set my book down on the desk, stood up and walked to the duty board. With a marker, I wrote next to my roommate's name the words "flight overdue." Then I turned, walked back to my desk, picked up the book and continued reading right where I'd left off. I simply *deadened myself* to the natural emotions I should have felt for my friend and fishing buddy.

The same sort of denial was evidenced by the gallows humor so common in the barracks. While a guy was dressing for a mission, his bunkmates would banter back and forth:

"If you buy the farm tonight, can I have your pillow?"

"No, I get his pillow. You can have his blanket."

"Hey, I asked first."

"Fine, take 'em both. But I get his flight jacket and his tape collection."

"No way. . . ."

Then the target of the razzing would walk out the door good-naturedly calling his friends vile names, and everyone would laugh about it.

We'd kidded Bob like that, the night his plane went down.

Of course, that kind of denial can't last forever. Laughing off the danger before your friends took off on a mission didn't change the terrible and sudden sensation of horror you felt when you awakened in darkness, rolled over in your bunk and groggily opened your eyes to see a bed that hadn't been slept in. You then had to will yourself back to sleep, forcing your eyes closed in the hope that the next time you opened them you'd see the familiar shape of a body, or even the reassuring sight of rumpled covers in the next bunk.

## Good Morning, Vietnam

Early in my tour I recognized a pattern on our base in DaNang, a rhythm of life echoed in the line from the Billy Joel song "Goodby Saigon," which says, "We ruled the day, but they ruled the night. And the night seemed as long as six weeks on Paris Island." There was a lot of truth to those lyrics. The level of fear seemed to rise with darkness and fall with daylight. Night was the time when the enemy moved. It was when the Vietcong launched mortar and rocket attacks. It was when you couldn't see what was coming from where. Because the A-6 had been designed specifically for night missions, most of my flights came after dark. So nightfall naturally brought a measure of anxiety as we anticipated our mission. It was during the night that my closest friends fought and sometimes died.

All of that probably explains why mornings were the best times in Vietnam. Six A.M. breakfasts were the most enjoyable meal of the day for me. I'd eat three-egg omelets oblivious to the dangers of cholesterol, knowing I'd survived a night of more immediate dangers and welcoming the early morning daylight that signaled another twelve-hour reprieve from darkness. Then I'd go back to my barracks and fall peacefully asleep, secure in the safety of daylight until darkness fell that night and the cycle began all over.

## No Time for Pretending

Ironically, despite the defense mechanisms which often prompted us to deny or ignore some of our deepest feelings, I believe combat duty to be as honest an environment as I've ever experienced. Façades crumble quickly in war. You are who you are and everyone knows it. If you're gutsy they know it. If you're a coward, they know that. If you're stupid they know it. And you know they know it.

I found it fascinating and sometimes tragic to witness the transformation that occurred when someone experienced the first shot fired at him in anger. In that one raw moment of fear all the pretenses of a lifetime instantly disappeared. I saw a number of salty career Marines, some of whom had risen to the rank of major without ever serving in a war zone, psychologically shattered by their first experience in combat. There seemed to be no way to accurately predict a person's reaction.

But as much as war teaches you about other people, it can teach you even more about yourself. And you may not like everything you learn.

I don't feel very good about the ease with which I shut off my emotions and so matter-of-factly wrote "flight overdue" on the board the night my roommate went down. Neither did I feel good about an embarrassing explosion of emotion I experienced around Christmastime 1967.

Bob Hope had come with his USO tour to hill 331 just outside DaNang. Raquel Welch was with him, wearing white boots and a skimpy red, white and blue outfit that made her look, from a distance, like a tightly rolled-up flag. But as much as we all appreciated the temporary diversion, that wasn't Christmas for me.

For me, Christmas that year was symbolized by the pile of presents Margaret Ann had sent me, shipping them early to make certain I received them in time. I'd immediately opened the packages containing perishable goodies and stacked the remaining boxes carefully on a chair next to my bed until Christmas Day. But one morning I came back from a mission to find that someone had evidently had too much to drink, staggered into our room by mistake, tipped over my bunk, bumped into the chair and scattered the presents across the floor.

It didn't bother me to have to set up and remake my bed, but when I saw those presents from my wife strewn over the floor, something inside me snapped. I started yelling, demanding to know who the culprit was and threatening to do him serious bodily harm. I was so suddenly, irrationally angry that I feel certain if I'd known who to go after I'd have tried to split his head open. But no one seemed to know who the tipsy visitor had been; at least no one said.

I awakened the next morning after a very fitful night's sleep feeling considerably calmer, but a little alarmed and chagrined about my overreaction the night before. By the time John, a guy I liked and respected, came by to apologize later that day, I shrugged the incident off and told him to forget it. Then, just to show him I had no lingering hard feelings, I scheduled myself to fly as his bombardier/navigator the next night.

I remember we had to dodge a SAM on that first mission. And from then on we felt so comfortable about our relationship that John and I chose to fly together at every opportunity—probably two hundred times or more before our tours ended. But the embarrassing incident that served as the catalyst for our strong and continuing friendship forced me to recognize my own startling capacity for sudden, irrational rage.

### A Baby Boy!

By no means was everything I learned about myself in Vietnam so negative. I vividly recall the explosion of instant joy I experienced the morning I walked into my room and spotted a Red Cross note stuck in the center of the tournament dart board Margaret Ann had sent to help me pass the waiting hours. The note, pinned up by a single dart, said simply:

Son Chris. Born 1/5/68. 8 lbs. 12 oz.

Mother and son doing fine.

Details came shortly in a letter from Margaret Ann detailing her thirty-six hours of difficult labor and including the first Polaroid pictures of our son. I showed the photos to everyone I knew and a few strangers besides. I even tucked them inside my flight suit to carry with me on my mission that night. When I peeled off the flight suit I found the photos sweat-soaked, stuck together and nearly ruined. But Margaret Ann kept me regularly supplied with new snapshots. Gradually the reality sank in and I began to feel something of this strange new sensation called fatherhood.

Over the following weeks my elation grew as I counted the days until I'd see my wife and meet my new son on my week-long R & R in Hawaii. But in the interim I was to encounter my single most significant personal experience of the war—an incident which challenged everything I believed and forced me to face the issues of life and death in terms I'd never considered before.

## Assignment: Death

It happened one day late in February. I remember sitting in the sunshine on top of a bunker reading the comics section of some Sunday newspaper when the duty officer for the day walked up and asked if I'd seen that night's target assignments yet. When I told him I hadn't he said, "You and John are going after Radio Hanoi."

The sound of his words hit me in the gut like a death sentence.

I understood the reasoning for the target. Just weeks before, Radio Hanoi had broadcast the signal that launched the infamous Tet Offensive of 1968. The most massive and coordinated enemy campaign of the war had simultaneously besieged American and South Vietnamese troops at numerous points throughout Vietnam, threatening briefly to overrun Saigon itself. Although our side had soon rallied and delivered what was probably the greatest single military victory of the entire war, Tet was in fact a resounding psychological, political and propaganda defeat for the American military.

After years of fighting, after the largest buildup of American forces since World War 2, and after months of assurances to Congress and the American public that victory was at hand, Tet proved to everyone that the end was not in sight, never had been—and perhaps never would be. The motive for bombing Radio Hanoi was purely revenge—payback from the American military and administrative leadership for the devastating embarrassment that was Tet.

And it was the most dangerous mission I could imagine. The thought of flying into downtown Hanoi, into the heart of what was probably the most extensive air defense system in the world at the time, filled me with paralyzing fear. Literally. I sat on that bunker for minutes, unable to move.

As a Christian, I'd always been quick to say, "I'm not afraid to die." I'd stand on my spiritual tiptoes and shout to anyone within earshot that you don't have to fear death if you know you're going to heaven and "to be absent from the body is to be present with the Lord."

But sitting alone on that bunker pondering my fate, I came to a humbling moment of realization. I suddenly understood that if, as Christians, we're not afraid to die, it is in large part because God in his great mercy hasn't told us when death will come. When we do know—whether it's six months from now, two days, or tonight over Hanoi—it challenges every scrap of faith we can muster.

I had no doubt. I knew that if I flew that mission I would die.

I finally managed to move off the bunker. But the fear and anxiety gripped me all day. The afternoon briefing only confirmed my fears. Ours would be one of two planes assigned to this mission. We would take off together and head north. When we reached the DMZ, the crew in the best position to continue, with the best-functioning equipment, would get the call and the other crew would break off and head for a secondary target far from Hanoi.

## "Don't Go!"

The pilot who briefed us on our assignments had attempted the same mission the week before. He'd had fifteen SAMs launched at him and had to abort his attack without ever getting within three miles of the target. He'd lit out of enemy territory the fastest way possible, but when he landed his bird in Thailand they counted fifteen different holes in the plane. He was going to receive the Silver Star just for *trying* the mission we were now assigned.

And this man told us the best possible advice he could give us was, "Don't go!"

That seemed like good advice to me. But none of us seriously considered the option of disobeying orders. And peer pressure combined with military discipline is a powerful motivator.

So the rest of the afternoon was spent poring over the maps and carefully plotting what I thought would be the safest route—as different as possible from the course that pilot had flown the week before. Finally there was nothing to do but wait until dark and time for takeoff. And to pray.

I routinely wrote Margaret Ann every day. That afternoon I didn't even try. I didn't know what to say; I certainly didn't want to put her through an emotional wringer by telling her about the agony of fear I was feeling on this last day of my life.

Finally the time came. And as I walked out to the plane and looked toward the mountains off to the west of the air base I remembered those words from the Psalms: "I lift up my eyes to the hills—where does my help come from? My help comes from the Lord, the Maker of heaven and earth" (Ps 121:1-2). The verses rang in my ears as I went through the pre-flight check of the bomb load. By the time I climbed into the cockpit to align the inertial navigational platform and feed the required data into the ballistics computer in final preparation for takeoff, I felt a little calmer.

I have to admit I gave all my equipment the toughest possible test. I bounced my radar from one side of its mount to the other; it still worked fine. The inertial guidance system, the most delicate and cantankerous instrument on the plane, was for once operating perfectly. John started the first engine, then the second. A careful double-check of all instruments showed no problem. Unfortunately, ours seemed to be the tightest bird imaginable.

But the familiar, routine procedures had a soothing effect. As we took off over the South China Sea and banked north, my anxiety level actually dropped. Even so, when the radio message came, it brought an intense sense of relief. Just as we neared the coast-in point where the decision had to be made as to which plane would go for Radio Hanoi, we got word our target had been changed. One of the electronic countermeasure aircraft assigned to provide cover for our mission, by flying high out over the sea and jamming the enemy radar for us, had developed mechanical trouble and had to turn back. With that development, the odds became so prohibitive that Central Control called off the Hanoi mission and sent us to drop our bombs on secondary targets just over the North Vietnamese border.

When I landed back in DaNang that night, it was with the exhilarating sense that I had somehow cheated death.

But the real lesson of the experience for me was the realization that when I had faced a fear more powerful than any emotion I'd ever known, in as honest a coming together of faith and fact as I could ever imagine, my faith had stood the test. I had sensed God's presence with me and a small measure of his peace.

The only down side of having our mission canceled was knowing that, since we'd already prepared for it, John and I would be the logical crew to draw the assignment next time.

However, all missions into the deep North were canceled later that spring, and with that change the danger level of our regular missions dropped considerably. For the first time, a thirteen-month tour seemed survivable.

When May came and my tour was more than half over, I spent

a glorious week of R & R in Hawaii getting reacquainted with my wife and finally meeting my four-month-old son. From then on I began to believe, really believe, that I was going to make it. I was going to come home from Vietnam.

# 4

# There's No Morality in War

What didn't survive the war was my innocence. My youthful naiveté and simplistic idealism. The black-and-white sense of values, the cut-and-dried, provincial view of the world I'd seen no reason to question while I was growing up in Harmony, New Jersey.

I can't say this loss was totally unexpected. In college I had a professor who came to teach at Brown after having served as the number two man in the CIA. He made a point that I never forgot when he said, "There is no morality in war." As a college student I hadn't understood all the implications of those words. As a soldier going into war I remembered them; I didn't arrive in Vietnam expecting or looking for morality. And indeed, what I found seemed to back up my professor's words.

Yet that didn't make the experience any less troubling.

## The Price of Stupidity

The first incident that drove home to me the point that there is no morality in war was the mission that cost the life of my roommate Steve. His was the second plane on a two-plane mission assigned to bomb a bridge over the Red River just outside Hanoi. The first plane made its run over the target, drawing heavy anti-aircraft and ground fire. Because the plane flew faster than the speed of sound, the enemy gunners fired into the black sky at the roar of the engines after that first jet was safely past. However, my roommate's plane, assigned to bomb the same target only seconds later, flew right into the flak, took a hit from a shell fired at the first plane, exploded and went down.

Where was the morality in that?

It was merely an ill-conceived mission that called for a totally unnecessary risk and caused the senseless deaths of two men. No matter that procedures were changed after that so that no plane would follow another so closely over a target. For two men and their families it was too late.

For countless men who died in Vietnam there were too many foolish plans and faulty strategies. The ultimate issue for them wasn't so much one of morality as of stupidity.

Steve's plane went down on October 31, 1967. The crew of the first plane saw the explosion of the second. It crashed on the outskirts of Hanoi. The North Vietnamese would have had the dog tags within hours. Yet they stashed the bodies of those fliers away to be used as bargaining chips nearly a decade after the American military role in Vietnam ended.

Steve's remains and those of the pilot were not returned until August 7, 1984. A three-year-old boy grew into a twenty-year-old man without ever knowing for sure that his father had died. A young wife lived for almost two decades with the uncertainty of her husband's fate. Where was the morality in that?

## Who Deserves What?

But before I condemn the immorality of the North Vietnamese, I have to consider what my response would be if another nation dropped bombs on *my* home for eight long years. We can rationalize our bombardment of North Vietnam by saying, "We were in the right, they were in the wrong—they deserved it." But I'm not sure the most aggressive army, let alone a civilian population, ever deserved that kind of continuous destruction year after year. Where's the morality when helpless women and children die by the tens of thousands?

If you look at any war through the grid of "morality" you'll find plenty of examples of injustice—some big and many small. Even the small ones can raise some pretty big *why* questions when you're getting shot at every day.

I remember landing in Thailand after a deep-North mission when we didn't think we had enough fuel to make it back to DaNang. Actually, we enjoyed an excuse to land at the U.S. air base in Thailand whenever we could as a break from the usual routine. Thailand had green grass where we had mud and sand. They had hot tubs; we had rocket attacks. They had air conditioning; we gratefully made do with wooden hooches which we considered a far cry better than the tents our Marine predecessors had used.

In the officers' club that night in Thailand, I talked with an Air Force flier who was celebrating his 100th combat flight because it qualified him to go home. I'd just come off my 134th mission and still had seven months of my tour to go because the Marine Corps didn't have any set number of missions that qualified a flier to be rotated home. I don't recall losing any sleep over that, but looking back it hardly seems fair.

That wasn't the only inequity Marines had to endure. Other branches of the service had one-year tours of duty in Vietnam. A Marine's tour lasted thirteen months. Some people joked that it was because the Marines thought there were thirteen months in a year. Perhaps it was just a policy of the Corps to show that Marines are a little tougher than everyone else. Whatever the reason, the result was that as Marines we had to stay and risk our lives longer than anyone else.

Then there was the issue of pay. As part of a Marine Expeditionary Force, we not only lived in inferior quarters, we also failed to qualify for temporary-duty pay. The Air Force personnel stationed with us at DaNang lived in better quarters just across the runway *and* they drew supplementary daily income for their "temporary duty" hardship.

We couldn't have done anything about these little injustices if we'd tried. But it didn't make any sense, and it clearly wasn't fair.

## Of Light and Lies

Truth, like fairness, is another frequent casualty of war. And any honest discussion of the "morality" (or lack thereof) of the Vietnam War has to acknowledge the damage done by the military's systematic policy of deceit. For years the military told the Congress and the American public what they wanted to hear.

"Give us a few thousand more men, a few more weapons, a few million more dollars and we'll win this war like we've won every other war we've ever fought. We have the enemy on the ropes, we're about to finish him off. We can see the light at the end of the tunnel." It was, as the title of war correspondent Neil Sheehan's book about the deceit suggests, *A Bright and Shining Lie*.

The public and Congress weren't the only ones being misled. Field officers were regularly pressured to lie to visiting brass. I remember being asked to brief a visiting general. "Tell him about all the Russian MIGs after us," I was instructed.

"But I've never seen a MIG," I countered.

"Well, some of the other guys have, so tell him. And be sure to tell him what it's like to have a bunch of SAMs shot at you!"

"I've only had one SAM launched at my plane."

"Well, it's happened to other guys. Tell him about it."

One reason the war lasted as long as it did and cost so many lives is that our American military failed to tell the truth. We hid so much for so long—such as the extent of drug problems and the frequency of the fragging incidents—that our deceit compounded the confusion, frustration and cynicism felt by those doing the fighting.

## Daylight, Death and Guilt

It's difficult to think of the morality of war without considering the moral implications of killing other human beings. I don't believe you can ever kill another person, whatever the circumstances, the reasons or the method, without losing something of yourself—your innocence, your idealism, your sensitivity—in the process.

In all honesty I can't say that I ever suffered a lot of guilt over my role in Vietnam. Maybe that's because fighting a war from the cockpit of an A-6 bomber at night is a pretty antiseptic experience. From all that I saw most nights—hunkered over a radar screen watching electronic pulses, arming the various weapons we carried, manning a computer—I could just as easily have been back in the States, sitting in a trainer, trying to put my cross hairs on a painted target.

A couple of exceptions stand out.

On Christmas Eve I flew a mission to hit a petroleum storage facility just outside of Vinh, the largest North Vietnamese town between the DMZ and Haiphong. I remember its being a beautiful moonlit night. We went in low and at the last second our ballistics computer malfunctioned. I called "Pickle!" to signal the pilot to manually release the bombs. But he dropped them just a little late. Looking back as we turned away and raced for home I saw our twenty-six 500-pound bombs explode in quick succession—ripping through the heart of the sleeping town. I felt sick knowing innocent people had died.

Another time, flying over South Vietnam in a rare daylight mission to provide air support for American ground troops, we swooped so low over an enemy stronghold that I could see Vietcong racing for a cluster of three bunkers. We dropped three 500-pound bombs. Looking back I saw them hit, one-two-three, each bomb plunging into a bunker and exploding. Three beautiful bull's-eyes.

Part of me felt a surge of elation at the precision of the feat. But another part of me cringed at the thought of the people who died in those bunkers—people who were real to me because I'd seen them in broad daylight, running and diving for cover just moments before our bombs blew them apart. For days afterwards, in my mind's eye I saw those people running. Their images remain vivid whenever I recall the incident more than twenty years later.

Yet, while at times I felt sadness and regret, I felt little or no guilt. Part of the reason, as I've said, is that I didn't usually witness death and destruction up close and personal. For as I've learned in more recent years, until you put a face on suffering, until you see the impact on individual human beings, it's easier just to deny your own responsibility, to avoid wrestling with your own reaction.

Another reason for my lack of guilt feelings was a deep sense of duty that went beyond my training as a Marine. I felt an undeniable obligation to the friends I served with, to the Corps, to my country, my family back home and everything I held dear.

Such a sense of duty-bound commitment was a very natural outgrowth of my conservative religious and patriotic upbringing. That background also contributed to the fact that even as a Christian with firm convictions about the sanctity of human life, I never felt inclined toward the intellectual pacifism subscribed to by so many in the sixties anti-war movement.

While I can't say I'd thought through all the implications of my view of war when I fought in Vietnam, I've wrestled with the subject since then. And I'd say my basic philosophical position hasn't changed much.

I could never be a pacifist because I know that at the ultimate point of implementation—if an enemy was coming over the wall with the intent of destroying my wife and children—I wouldn't hesitate to pull the trigger. Knowing I couldn't be a pacifist at that ultimate point, I cannot with any sense of integrity claim to be an intellectual pacifist.

If you divide people into three broad groups based on their view of war—pacifists; those who believe in limited, just wars; and those who would advocate the all-out use of nuclear weapons to achieve victory—I'd have to place myself in the middle group. (Even though I theoretically have to say that there can be such a thing as a just war, I don't know that nuclear war and the resulting destruction could ever be considered "just.")

And in real life, I've seen enough destruction—in Vietnam as a Marine, and much more since, visiting Vietnam, Thailand, Afghanistan, Mozambique, Sudan and other hot spots in connection with World Vision—to understand the horror of war. You have only to see the suffering so visible in any refugee camp or VA hospital to realize there is really no such thing as a "just" war. The terrible price of war is so great that no one ever wins; when we resort to war to settle our problems, everyone loses. Some just lose more than others.

Understanding that, I'm very much against war. And yet, I still place myself in that middle group. I believe there are times when war may become necessary to right an even bigger wrong. As terrible as the price is, and we must never lose sight of that cost, I believe there are some things in life worth fighting for, even worth dying for. And my experiences in Vietnam, both during the war and more recently, have brought focus and awareness of some of those most critical values.

## Two Who Didn't Have to Die

In recent years I've become friends with a man who was in charge of the Christian Missionary and Alliance denomination's mission work in Vietnam during the late sixties. He told me the story of four American missionaries, two men and two women, living in a Vietnamese village near the Laotian border around the time I was stationed in Vietnam. Their denomination encouraged them to leave, but they all chose to stay and continue their ministry—preaching, teaching, nursing and living out a gospel of hope in the midst of a chaotic war. Whenever fighting spilled over into their region, these missionaries would leave their village and hide out in the surrounding jungle until the danger passed.

One day the two men were on a trail outside the village when they spotted a band of North Vietnamese regulars approaching. They tried to run and warn the others, but they'd been seen and were captured. Their shoes were taken from them; one man's glasses were torn from his face, thrown on the ground and trampled. Then they were tied to a tree and threatened with death for spying.

In the meantime, some of the North Vietnamese troops continued into the village where the two women, with no chance to escape to the jungle, had barely enough time to slip out of sight and hide inside a house. But the soldiers soon found them there, dragged them outside, tied them up under the house and set it on fire, burning the two missionary women to death.

The two men, knowing nothing of their colleagues' fate, remained under guard, tied to that tree in the jungle. An elderly man from the village, learning of their capture, rushed out to where they were held and begged their captors to let them go. He tried to explain that the missionaries weren't spies; they had just come to his village to help teach the people and tell them about Jesus.

"They are good men. Let them go."

The guards, waving their AK-47s, threatened the old man and

ordered him to leave. Instead, he walked over to the men and began untying them. The guards knocked the old man down, but they didn't kill him. And they didn't kill the missionaries either. They marched the two barefoot Americans through the jungle for weeks, north along the Ho Chi Minh trail to Hanoi. Years later, near the end of the war when the North Vietnamese released the POWs held in the Hanoi Hilton, among them were these two men.

Hearing their story greatly moved me. Perhaps that was because I'd been in Vietnam during the same time. I may have flown right over them or even dropped bombs around them without ever knowing they were there.

I was a Christian; I was there out of duty to my country. I couldn't leave for thirteen months. I suspect they too felt a sense of duty, but they were serving under a different set of orders. They certainly didn't have to stay there. But they chose to remain because of what they believed. They decided their faith was worth dying for if necessary. And that decision cost two of them their lives and the others years of suffering.

Their example challenges me. It forces me to consider seriously the question: "Do I really believe my faith is worth dying for?"

I want to say yes. But their story convicts me because it forces me to recall one of the most painful failures of my own life as a Christian. It too happened in Vietnam.

### Failing My Friend—and My Faith
Jim Fickler was one of the pilots in our squadron and the best friend I had during my stint in the Marines. We'd met during training at Cherry Point. When he arrived in DaNang a few weeks after me, I was glad for the chance to renew and build on our friendship.

Jim had the kind of warm, open personality that made everybody like him. He probably wasn't the world's best pilot—I remember he even lost a plane taking off over the bay one day—but I enjoyed flying with him because he was steady and unflappable. A solid guy you could count on to do the right thing at the right time.

We quickly learned we had a lot in common. We both owned hunting dogs. He trained Labrador retrievers back home in Wisconsin; I trained setters. We both loved to hunt and fish and we'd trade stories by the hour—the fish getting just a little bigger and the deer a little swifter with each telling. Jim was an accomplished sportsman; at the age of twenty-six he'd already bagged more than two dozen deer and landed thirty-seven muskellunge.

Whenever we could arrange an assignment to fly one of the planes to the Philippines for maintenance and washing, we'd try to go together. The flight was just nine hundred miles due east, and we'd share a day or two of R & R at the base on Cubi Point. You could get a shave, a massage, a shampoo and a manicure for $1.98. And we'd shoot skeet.

As the months wore on we developed an honest-to-goodness, once-in-a-lifetime friendship. We talked for hours about our plans after the war. We dreamed of finding some land in the Midwest and creating our own shooting preserve. Whatever we did, we planned to keep in touch.

I left Vietnam a few weeks before Jim's tour was up. I'd only been back in the States four or five weeks when I heard. He'd been shot down over Laos and was presumed dead.

The news hit me like a body blow to the gut. Jim dead.

I retraced every conversation we ever had, all the issues we ever talked about, all the plans we made, all the dreams we shared. And to my everlasting shame I couldn't remember one conversation in which I had told him about my faith.

I think of those missionaries who decided their faith was worth dying for. And in all those months I hadn't considered my faith worth sharing with my best friend.

Christians call the gospel the Good News. If we believe it's good news, if it's the most important thing in our lives, how can we not share it?

I don't know what Jim believed. I don't know where he was spiritually when he died. But I knew he was dead, dead without ever hearing from my lips any talk about something more important than our dreams of the future, something more transcendent than the war.

I knew I would live with that regret forever. I vowed not to make the same mistake ever again. And whenever I've had an opportunity, I've told the story of Jim Fickler in the hopes that hearing about my failure may prevent someone else from making the same mistake.

## Coming Home

I was one of the fortunate ones in Vietnam. My tour of duty provided me with what was certainly the single richest year of experience in my life. It matured me. It taught me much about myself, my faith.

I survived, and my marriage survived, though I came home from Vietnam needing to relearn what it was like to be a husband, and to learn how to be a father. It wasn't the easiest adjustment; for a while, I was the one adult in my son's life who would make him cry just by picking him up.

It took a while for us to get to know each other. But I soon enjoyed being a dad. And the following year our daughter, Amy, was born at Cherry Point where I served out the remainder of my Marine Corps duty as an instructor for other bombardier/navigators.

Fatherhood the second time around was a wonderful improvement over the initial experience. Instead of learning about the birth secondhand, thousands of miles away, I was there. I experienced the miracle of new life. And the incredible nature of love. How I could love Margaret Ann and Chris with all my heart and being, only to have my capacity for love instantly increased by another fifty per cent with the birth of a beautiful daughter I loved every bit as much—that for me was a miracle.

There was much to learn about love, family and the joys of parenting. And intertwined with all that was the need to make decisions about life after the Marines.

For a year I sold building supplies; my sales territory covered the western half of Michigan's lower peninsula. During that year I learned I had natural sales ability, but I also decided I didn't want to spend my life selling inanimate objects.

From there I went back to Brown to work in the admissions department for a year and a half before becoming assistant athletic director.

From the time I'd played football in college, I had dreamed of someday being the athletic director of a Division I school. At the age of thirty-two I achieved that goal at my own alma mater. I found it to be a terrific job that enabled me to work with a lot of wonderful people. But at the age of thirty-five I realized my emotional highs and lows were being determined by how a bunch of nineteen-year-old kids played in a game on Saturday afternoons.

I realized there had to be more important things to do in the eternal scope of things. Something was out of kilter when I experienced more feeling at a football game than I did in a church service.

So I asked the president of Brown University for a position with the school's new fund-raising program. Eventually he named me as vice president for development and put me in charge of a five-year, $158-million capital campaign. I'd never done any fund-raising, so taking the assignment looked like a huge risk. But I accepted the challenge partly because it was a challenge, and partly because I felt a call.

We raised $182 million, not $158 million, in five years. During the final months of the campaign, when I knew we'd surpass our goal, I looked around and realized that with the campaign over, the next year was going to seem pretty dull. So I began considering what I would do next.

At this point in my life, my thinking and my plans for the future were being influenced greatly by my spiritual values. While I've been a Christian my entire adult life, it wasn't until I was in my mid-thirties that I began to understand how much the Bible has to say about our obligation to others, about how Christians need to be putting faith into practice every day—personally and corporately. So it was that I accepted a call to become president of Eastern College and Eastern Baptist Theological Seminary in St. Davids, Pennsylvania—two institutions with a single purpose summed up in the motto: "The whole Gospel for the whole world."

Over the next few years I gained new insights into the meaning of that motto. As I studied the Bible and read books by Christian authors who wrote about the impact our faith should have on our relationship to others, the gospel message seemed to grow somehow larger and richer. I began to understand that Jesus was more than an example of God's grace; he was also a model of responsibility and identification with a broken world.

Too often we've tried to dichotomize the "liberal" social gospel of action from the "conservative" gospel of personal repentance and salvation. The world desperately needs both. For just as Easter without Good Friday is only half the gospel, Good Friday without Easter is no gospel at all.

At the time I became president of two institutions of higher learning, I didn't hold a graduate degree. I wasn't an ordained minister. I wasn't even the right kind of Baptist (in this case, American Baptist). But again I felt called to accept the challenge.

I spent four wonderful years at Eastern. There I interacted with a lot of stimulating people—thinking Christians like Tony Campolo and Ron Sider. I didn't always agree with everything they said, but they taught me much about Christian concern and compassion. They showed me the importance of learning to see the world not just with my eyes, but with my heart.

The lessons learned in my years at Eastern prompted me to accept yet another challenge in 1987 when I was asked to become president of World Vision, Inc. And it is that role that took me back to Vietnam, this time with a very different agenda: to help achieve something positive there, to do something right in a country where I felt I accomplished so little during the war.

I would quickly add that my motivation is not prompted by feelings of guilt regarding my role during the war. World Vision has gotten involved in Vietnam because, in the great landscape of a world littered with bodies, Vietnam is one of those places that needs help. Yet I do have a special interest in Vietnam because of the role it played in my own life and in the development of my own values.

**Vietnam: Right or Wrong?**
I can't conclude this chapter, with all the talk about Vietnam's impact on my own values, my view of war, and the lack of morality in war without acknowledging that I've intentionally avoided discussing the validity of America's involvement in Vietnam. The debate over this issue divided America for years in a way our nation hadn't been divided since the Civil War. Historians may continue to debate it forever.

Having gained a firsthand view of postwar Vietnam, I would have a more difficult time than ever saying that all of us who fought and all those who died in Vietnam were wrong to oppose the North Vietnamese. The eventual communist takeover resulted in terrible and untold suffering for millions of people.

And yet, when I look at the results of the war, and the terrible price paid on both sides of the Pacific, I can build a pretty strong case against American involvement in Vietnam. Certainly our strategy was wrong, not just faulty but futile.

Given the world of the fifties and early sixties, and given the fact that America had never lost a war and much of our foreign policy was predicated on that record, one could then argue that the war was inevitable. Certainly it was understandable—everything from the military reaction to the public reaction to the way the politicians shifted their positions. Looking at it in context, Vietnam seems very understandable. And forgivable—inasmuch as people feel the need for forgiveness.

However, it is not my intent to argue for or against America's role in the Vietnam War. There is really nothing to be gained. In the remainder of this book I'm much more concerned with what has happened since America pulled out of Vietnam in 1975. For I believe that when we consider the evidence, all of us, whatever our view on the Vietnam War—liberal or conservative, hawk or dove, Democrat or Republican—should agree that what has happened since 1975 has been very wrong. It's why the wounds of Vietnam remain open and raw a generation later. It's why the Vietnam War is still a war without closure.

# Part II
## A War Without Closure

# 5
# The Missing . . . and the Hidden Casualties

The most poignant reminder that the Vietnam War remains a "war without closure" is the issue of America's MIAs. Another proof of this ongoing pain came in the summer of 1991 with the release of a photo from undercover sources purporting to show three American military men, lost since the sixties—still alive in Southeast Asia.

Whether or not that controversial photo was authentic, whether or not any of the countless rumors or "reports" which continue to filter out of Southeast Asia are true, such information serves as salt in the open wounds of MIA families.

For although two decades have passed since U.S. troops pulled out of Vietnam, there remain over two thousand men—brothers, sons, husbands, fathers—officially listed as "Missing in Action."

I've made the acquaintance of a remarkable woman by the name of Ann Mills Griffiths who heads up the League of Families, a nationwide organization composed of relatives of MIAs who offer each other support and information and who lobby the government for help and resolution on the MIA issue. I try to meet with Ann whenever I'm in Washington. I brief her on my recent trips back to Vietnam; I read the League's newsletter regularly. I want to do all I can, personally and within World Vision, to offer information and help to these bereaved families who live with the open wound of uncertainty about the fate of those they love.

**"Overdue"**

The MIA issue arouses powerful feelings within me because it's been very personal to me—on two different levels.

I was once designated as MIA. It's there, though just a minor footnote, in the official Marine Corps history as recorded in the VM (AW) 242 log book: Capt. Robert Seiple is listed as "Missing in Action."

It happened one night in the spring of 1968. We were assigned a target just over the border in North Vietnam. Central Control reported a lot of SAM activity in the area, and just as we were about to go "feet dry" our airborne controllers were informed that an Air Force F-4 had gone down, the two fliers had ejected and were now afloat in the South China Sea. Since ours was the closest plane, we were ordered to fly RESCAP. So we quickly dropped our bombs, pulled off our planned return course and headed out to sea.

Our job was simple. We throttled back the engines to conserve fuel. Then we flew a slow, lazy racetrack pattern around and around the downed fliers to reassure them someone was there and help was on its way. We were nothing more than a morale booster. With no offensive weapons aboard, there was nothing we could do to protect them should enemy planes or boats appear—unless we got desperate enough to pull back the canopy and start firing our .38 pistols.

All in all, it was an incredibly boring flight. Around and around. An hour passed as we waited for rescue craft to arrive. Two hours. We'd been strapped into our seats for so long my legs began to cramp. Four long hours passed before Central Command thanked us and sent us home.

What we didn't know was that all the time we'd been flying RESCAP, our squadron had been getting more and more concerned. We'd been unable to sign off our original radio frequency before we had to switch channels to listen to the voice contact between the downed pilots and control. In the confusion, no one but the airborne controllers knew where we were.

All our squadron knew was that our target had been in North Vietnam, there'd been a lot of SAMs fired earlier, our fuel supply should have been gone by then, and our flight was listed on the Operations Room assignment board as "overdue."

So our friends and colleagues were preparing to take their planes up at first light to look for us when we walked into the operations room, relaxed and joking.

I can't adequately describe the reception we got—the wondrous welcome we saw on the faces and heard in the words of our colleagues. Some of the men in that group I liked very much; others weren't so close. Some I shared much in common with; others were very different from me. But when we walked into that room alive, I felt an incredible, instant embrace of friendship. I felt like Lazarus back from the grave, or maybe like Tom Sawyer happening upon his own funeral. This wonderful realization that people cared, that my life mattered that much to my colleagues, was terribly affirming.

My own MIA experience had a happy ending. It was over so quickly my family didn't have to be notified. But the experience has forced me to consider how my loved ones would have reacted if I hadn't returned. And I think it has given me an extra measure of empathy for MIAs' families.

## Crosses on the Wall

But there's a second reason the MIA issue triggers such feelings within me. Every name I know which is etched into that black marble wall of the Vietnam War Memorial has a cross after it—signifying "Missing in Action." I never experienced the horror of the ground war where a buddy might get shot, fall in the mud beside you and die in your arms. An air war provides another kind of horror where a friend simply climbs into his plane, disappears up into the night sky . . . and never returns. So I never had to haul a friend's body across swamps and through the jungle to an evacuation point. But I had to carry a different kind of burden—an uncertainty that both blurred the reality of death and prolonged the grief by denying me any clear sense of finality.

For more than twenty years now, whenever MIAs or their families are mentioned in the media, I remember the faces of my two roommates, of my best friend Jim Fickler, and of the others from my squadron who disappeared and died somewhere in the sea, the sky or the jungles of Southeast Asia. Whenever there's a news report of more bodies being found, more remains being returned by the Vietnamese government, I listen for the names. And as I wait for word I think of the families who wait and wonder and pray and even still hope.

## Steve and Jim Come Home

I remember August 7, 1984. I was on vacation, bass fishing in the Poconos. I picked up a copy of *USA Today* and learned five more bodies had been released. I scanned down through the article to learn two were Marines. Then I saw the names—my roommate Steve and his pilot, Jim, the ones who had gone down in the flak trap on that ill-conceived mission outside Hanoi.

Seeing those familiar names instantly resurrected the vivid memories of two young faces and a reservoir of feelings I'd dammed up inside nearly half my life. The article said Jim's son was now twenty. He'd been three when Jim had gone down. Seventeen years! As I did the simple math, a jumble of thoughts raced through my mind: *Jim's boy is that old? It's been that long? What does that do to a family? A whole generation lost! There are two thousand more families out there still waiting! It just goes on and on! Why?*

For me, the MIAs and their families have always been the most eloquent reminders that Vietnam was and is a war without closure.

## The Hidden Casualties

But they certainly aren't the only reminders. More than two and a half million American men and women returned from service in Vietnam. And in a very real way, every one of us is living proof of that war's continuing impact.

I doubt that anyone who has fought in a war, any war in the history of the world, has ever "gotten over" the experience. The images, the events and the emotions can never be fully forgotten; their influence on a survivor's identity can never be escaped.

Every war has had its physically wounded. Bodies were broken and limbs severed by ancient battle-axes, though far less efficiently and in fewer numbers than by claymore mines. The inhabitants manning the walls of medieval castles poured boiling oil down on their attackers; today's planes spew napalm from the sky. Plagues and disease have long been part of war's terrible aftermath, though the time bomb called Agent Orange brought a terrible twentieth-century twist.

And every war has its emotionally wounded. One of the oldest, most common human coping mechanisms for surviving war is to detach yourself from your emotions. I've heard the advice countless times: "Try not to feel. Don't let yourself get too close to your men." We tell this to those we send off to war, for the most part young people at the point in their development when they're just beginning to understand the emotional maze of their humanity. We expect them to develop the psychological survival skill of denying or shutting down their most basic and natural human emotions; then we wonder why so many of them come home emotionally missing in action, psychologically handicapped and unable to find the handle controlling the faucet that will open the normal flow of healthy, human feelings again.

Certainly Vietnam created the kind of lasting physical and emotional wounds that war veterans have always suffered. But the Vietnam vets' experience was different—and in at least one way worse. Because the healing embrace of home and country wasn't there when we returned.

To be sure, most of us were welcomed home by open-armed families. But that was often the extent of any positive reception.

As Pierre Salinger, press secretary to presidents Kennedy and Johnson, observed in a recent *American Heritage* article, "[Vietnam] was the first war in the history of the United States in which the veterans who returned home were not considered heroes, and it was the first war in the history of the United States that did not have vast public support."

But it went beyond apathy or lack of support. Veterans returned from Vietnam to face harsh opposition, criticism and in many cases personal condemnation for their service.

### Coming Home to Hurt
The intensity of their resulting pain was powerfully documented in Chicago Tribune columnist Bob Greene's book *Homecoming: When the Soldiers Returned from Vietnam.* For years Greene had heard stories that when American troops returned home from Vietnam they were spat upon by anti-war protesters. The stories were usually very similar and very specific. A soldier, in uniform and fresh off the plane from Vietnam, was walking through the airport when he

encountered a bunch of "hippies" who spat on him.

Greene had heard the stories so many times that he wondered about their veracity. One day he raised the subject in his syndicated column and asked readers to respond to the question, "Did this ever really happen?"

The overwhelming response shocked Greene. More than a thousand people sent letters telling about their homecoming experiences—negative and positive. When Greene selected a handful of letters to excerpt over several days in his column, he got a second wave of response as people phoned and wrote to tell him of their emotional reaction to reading the letters.

What started as an idea for a newspaper column provided more than enough material for a book. *Homecoming* is a selection of letters Bob Greene received. Enough people told of being spat upon to convince Greene that the stories actually happened—again and again. But as Greene wrote in his introduction, "Many more [letters], though, said that the question—if taken literally—was irrelevant. They said it didn't matter whether a civilian actually worked up sputum and propelled it toward them—they said they were made to feel small and unwanted in so many other ways that it felt like being spat upon. . . . Many of the veterans prefaced their letters by saying that they had never before revealed their feelings on the subject. Their emotions ran so deep, they had never wanted to tell anyone."

I was never spat upon. And I'd probably have decked anyone who tried.

I'd say I was fairly well sheltered from the anti-war sentiment while I was in the service. I do remember the surprise and shock I felt one day in Vietnam when I picked up a copy of *Newsweek* featuring campus protests, with a cover shot of radicals who had taken over Cornell University's administration building. Right there in the cover photo was a fist-waving protester wearing bandoliers across his chest like some sort of campus guerrilla. I remember thinking, "I'm over here fighting a war so guys like that have the freedom to take over college administration buildings?"

So I was, of course, aware of the opposition to the war. But even once I was back in the States completing my tour of duty, I didn't experience such sentiment firsthand. It was only after I got out of the service and back in the academic setting on a university campus that the lack of objectivity and balance concerning the war made me feel out of place and devalued for my role.

### A Lasting Judgment?

Those feelings didn't fade with the ebb of the anti-war movement or the end of the war. I doubt they did for most Vietnam vets.

How often over the years have we heard references to the "tragedy of Vietnam," the "mistake of Vietnam" or similar phrases?

More than twenty years later, a CBS/New York Times poll indicated only fourteen per cent of the U.S. population thought the country "did the right thing" in Vietnam as compared with seventy-seven per cent who thought the U.S. should have stayed out. A series of ten different opinion polls—the first in April 1965 and the last in March 1985, ten years after the fall of Saigon—shows a constant, steady increase in the percentage of Americans agreeing with the statement "Vietnam was a mistake."

Can any veteran help feeling belittled, tainted or labeled by our connection to a war so viewed? Numerous times over the years I've had people ask me, "Were you a Christian when you fought in Vietnam?" The unspoken assumption is that a Christian certainly wouldn't have participated in the "tragedy of Vietnam."

There has been an attempt more recently, as evidenced even by those few protesting against the war in the Persian Gulf, to differentiate between criticism of our government's war policy and the soldiers who carry it out. But I'm afraid such careful, targeted criticism comes too late for most Vietnam vets. For more than two decades the implication of American public opinion was painfully clear: "If the war was wrong, so were those who fought it."

Even for those veterans who stand by their original convictions and don't believe the war was wrong, it's an inescapable fact that at some point someone made the decision, which our government then acted upon, that *the Vietnam War wasn't worth it anymore*. And then the pullout began.

That decision had an immediate and lasting impact on everyone who served in Vietnam. For those who died, it meant they paid the ultimate price for something eventually deemed worthless. Their sacrifice was in vain. For those who survived the war, it meant our suffering and sacrifice were ultimately pointless. And every Vietnam-related headline, every news report out of Southeast Asia is another stabbing reminder of the futility of our generation's war.

As our efforts are devalued, so are we. The resulting sense of alienation and pain manifests itself in a great many ways. Consider the above-average divorce rate among Vietnam vets; the high rate of alcoholism and drug abuse; the estimated 7,000-8,000 vets living as recluses in mountains and woods of the American Northwest; the continuing phenomenon psychiatrists have named "post-Vietnam stress syndrome" which continues to devastate individuals, marriages and families twenty years and more after the war.

Even for those whose wounds have begun to heal, the pain and the feelings remain close to the surface. I see the evidence in the incredible outpouring of emotion in Bob Greene's book. I see it in the way Vietnam memories can instantly trigger my own deepest feelings.

The pain is still there for most of us Vietnam vets because we feel the lack of closure. And our society hasn't done much to help. For years it was as if Americans had collective amnesia—Vietnam was so quickly and easily forgotten. Perhaps it was a kind of collective post-Vietnam stress syndrome we were suffering through.

There *has* been a gradual change in recent years, a shift in attitude toward those who served in Vietnam. The evidence is there: at the Vietnam War Memorial in Washington, D.C.; in the box-office success of movies such as *Platoon* and *Full Metal Jacket;* in the popularity of TV shows such as "Tour of Duty" and "China Beach." In the wake of the Persian Gulf War, the organizers of some victory parades included Vietnam vets as well as Gulf War troops.

So the public perception of Vietnam vets may be changing. But it seems clear to me that most Vietnam vets are still missing the peace that can come only from a healthy sense of closure.

Can we ever have that closure? Will we ever, for the sake of the MIAs and those who came home, find the missing peace?

I believe it's possible. And we'll talk about how it could happen in Section III of this book. But first we're going to consider some others who continue to be victims of a war without closure.

# 6
## The Children
## We Left
## Behind

When the last American helicopter pulled out of Vietnam on April 30, 1975, the end came quickly. So quickly, in fact, that much was left behind. Personal belongings, war machines—and American blood; sunbaked on the stained courtyard of the Temple of Harmony at Hue. Diluted in the rivers of the Mekong Delta. Shrouded beneath the brush of the Annamese Cordillera. But that is the blood of the dead, the blood of American men who were mourned and memorialized on a granite wall in Washington, D.C. Less remembered is the blood left behind in more than 30,000 living memorials called Amerasians: the children of American men, including servicemen and civilians, and Asian women."—*World Vision* Magazine, Aug/Sept 1990

How many movies, TV shows and stories have been written over the years with a plot line fantasizing about some daring Rambo-style raid into Southeast Asia to rescue American MIAs still being held alive in some remote jungle prison camp? The slowly fading hopes of our entire nation find expression in such fiction. For more than two decades Americans have waited and watched and worked to discover the fate of our MIAs—the family members we were forced to leave behind.

Amerasians are the family members we *chose* to leave behind. For twenty years we've known who they are, where they are and the terrible suffering they've endured. Yet we've done little or nothing to rescue them.

### Face to Face

I knew about the Amerasians in Vietnam before my first postwar visit to that country in 1988. I'd read articles written by Western correspondents and seen the photo features in American magazines. But nothing had prepared me for the face-to-face encounters with so many Amerasian young people on the streets of Ho Chi Minh City that very first night back "in country."

In the initial excitement of our arrival in Vietnam, and in an attempt to soak in the ambience of the city, Margaret Ann, Jesse and I waved down a cyclo (one of those bicycle-buggies that serve as human-powered taxis in much of Southeast Asia) outside our hotel and hired the driver to take us on an early evening tour of the town.

We spotted them everywhere we went in the city. Their unmistakably American features stood out amidst the swirling sea of Asian faces surging up and down the crowded streets.

They were as attracted to us as we were to them. We too stood out on those streets—an American family, a blonde woman and a sandy-haired kid. We looked like them. They looked like us. There was a visual connection, an instant identity there.

It was when we tried to communicate that we were struck by a surprising dissonance. They looked so clearly Western, their eyes rounder, their noses larger, their skin lighter (or in some cases darker) than the other faces around us. Yet they sounded unmistakably Asian. The combination made them seem both American and Vietnamese—and perhaps, sadly, neither.

Amerasians gathered around us wherever we went that night and every time we ventured out into the streets in the days that followed. The few who knew a smattering of English words were always anxious to try them out on us.

"What's your name?" one young girl asked.

"Bob," I replied.

"That's my father's name too," she said wistfully. She didn't know his last name. Or where in the States he lived.

## The Price of American Blood

The one I remember best was Mai, a twenty-year-old with a slight Vietnamese build who might have passed for thirteen. A beautiful young woman whose name translates "Flower," Mai didn't speak English. But when we met she looked deep into my eyes, hoping to see the face of her long-lost father. I learned that she regularly went to the airport to meet any incoming international flight, in hopes of seeing her returning father step off the plane. Her only real memory of her father comes from a worn photograph which once belonged to her mother. She carries that image permanently etched in her mind wherever she goes.

For me, Mai's freckled face and her ongoing search epitomized the sad plight of the Amerasians in Vietnam. Like many if not most Amerasians in Vietnam, Mai made her living on the streets. They sell stamps and maps to foreigners. They beg for things like soap and shampoo—commodities they can turn around and sell for ready cash. They are the poorest of the poor in an impoverished land. The Vietnamese term for them, *bui doi,* means "the dust of life."

They are nothing. They live in the country that won the war, but the Amerasians themselves are perhaps the biggest losers.

In a culture which prides itself on its ethnic purity, the obvious Black or White features of young Amerasians burden them with a double stigma. Not only is their blood tainted, but they are a living reminder to the Vietnamese of their own painful losses in the war. Their faces look too much like the faces of the enemy to ever forget—or forgive. And these children left behind by the enemy are no longer cute little toddlers. They've grown up to be young men and young women, now the same age as (and perhaps too much like) their fathers who came to fight a war.

Despite rumors to the contrary, the communist government of Vietnam never established any official policy of retribution against these *bui doi*. But they didn't really have to. Culturally accepted discrimination is an unavoidable fact of Amerasian life. Many mothers of Amerasian children were blocked from decent-paying jobs. Teachers as well as students often taunted Amerasian children as *my lai*—half-breed. Many Amerasians have been deprived of local government benefits, whether educational or medical.

One Vietnamese mother of a mixed-blood daughter said, "She was terribly sick, vomiting blood. The people at the hospital refused to treat her, saying, 'She is American. Let the Americans cure her!' "

Many mothers wanted to flee with their Amerasian children, but severed diplomatic ties with the West made emigration impossible for years. And illegal escapes to other countries were terribly dangerous.

Other survival strategies became necessary. Many Amerasians abandoned city residence for a less troubled life in the remote countryside. Some mothers took more drastic measures. "I dyed my daughter's hair with black shoe polish, put soot on her face and cut off her eyelashes," one mother recalled. "And I kept her hidden under a blanket all the time in the house."

## Forgotten Families

The Amerasian children in Vietnam, and the mothers who bore and loved them, were pretty much left to their own resources. They had few advocates within, and received little help from, our American government. For years we even downplayed the problem by underestimating the number of Amerasians. Despite claims from reputable sources like the Pearl S. Buck Foundation and others that the Amerasians and their immediate families numbered upwards of 150,000, the State Department only acknowledged there might be 10-15,000.

And when Congress finally passed a bill in 1982 granting visa preference to Amerasians, the State Department didn't apply the policy because there was still no provision for the Vietnamese family and relatives of Amerasians; few were willing to emigrate alone. And since there were no diplomatic ties between Vietnam and the U.S., any Amerasian wanting to leave Vietnam had to take the risk of declaring his intentions, apply to leave, and suffer the indignities and expense inflicted by a hostile bureaucracy with no assurance he'd be allowed to leave.

If he got permission, he then had to go through a U. N. refugee process and finally provide some sort of documentation to the U.S. immigration officials to prove he was who he claimed to be.

When the French left Vietnam in 1954, they took 25,000 mixed Vietnamese/French children back to Europe and offered them all French citizenship when they turned eighteen. In contrast, Americans not only left the Amerasian children behind, but we actually raised diplomatic barriers to hinder their escape.

And just as our government failed to address the Amerasian issue, so did the American public. Unlike the MIAs, there were no groups orchestrating support for Amerasians or demanding that Vietnam give a full accounting of every Amerasian before we would ever consider diplomatic recognition or an end to economic sanctions.

Most disturbing of all is the evident disinterest of the fathers. According to the Amerasian Registry and the Pearl S. Buck Foundation (which assists children of mixed American and Asian heritage), fewer than five hundred American GIs have ever made official inquiries about their Amerasian children.

How can we explain the fathers' silence?

Perhaps they lost hope as the years passed. Maybe they figured the communist victory precluded any possibility that their children had survived or could get out. Some may have rationalized that any efforts on their part might further endanger their children's tenuous predicament.

But none of this explains why, in the relatively few cases where Amerasians finally cleared all the emigration hurdles and officials have been able to identify and contact fathers, the majority of fathers have said they want no contact with their offspring. The sad fact is, it wasn't uncommon for such notations to be included in veterans' service records. And their emigrating Amerasian children and their mothers were never told.

How do we explain this? Guilt. Selfishness. Embarrassment. Fear of having a new life complicated, an American wife and children compromised.

Can there be any adequate justification for the suffering endured by the Amerasian children we left behind in Vietnam?

### Two War Babies

No doubt one reason Mai's story speaks so to me is because I can't think of her without thinking about my own son, Chris.

Both Mai and Chris were war babies. Both were born in 1968. Both of their fathers were American servicemen. They might have had so much in common. Yet their lives could hardly have been more different.

Chris grew up in America with a smorgasbord of opportunities so often taken for granted in the richest, most powerful nation in the world. He had all the benefits of our educational and health care system. His life was crammed full of learning experiences—travel, association with a wide range of interesting people, constant exposure to information and the broader world through newspapers, magazines, books and the electronic media. He was one of the world's privileged minority of middle-class America—the nation that "lost" the Vietnam War.

Mai grew up in the country that "won" the war. She received no health care, no education; she can't even read her native language of Vietnamese. She survived on the streets of Saigon, begging and scavenging for castoff items to sell so she could buy food. And she went to the airport whenever she could to meet incoming flights— day after day, week after week, month after month, year after year— in the hope that her father might someday return for her.

Perhaps it was that hope which enabled her to survive. She had little else.

In the spring of 1990, when I visited Mai for the third time on my third trip back to Vietnam, she had just gotten clearance to emigrate to America as part of the Vietnam government's "Orderly Departure Program" and the U.S. government's Amerasian Homecoming Act. She didn't know when she would finally be able to leave for the refugee orientation center in the Philippines, but she insisted she'd be ready to go at a moment's notice. All that she owned, every possession she had to show for her twenty-two years of earthly existence, she had carefully packed in one shoe box which she would carry with her to begin a new life on the other side of the world.

I couldn't help but think of Chris who drove back and forth to college in his own car, packed to overflowing with all the "things" the average American kid has in more abundance than Mai could have imagined in her wildest fantasies.

What incredibly different lives these two children of American fathers have lived! The greater tragedy is that these same differences can be found, this same disturbing parallel drawn, for every one of thousands of Amerasian young people.

I happened to be ten thousand miles away when Chris was born. He had to wait ten months for his dad to return. But when I came back from Vietnam I became a father in earnest. I watched proudly and gratefully as Chris grew up. We fished and hunted together. I was overwhelmed with joy when, as a boy, he accepted Christ as his personal Lord and Savior. I cheered as he became a high-school Regional All-American in soccer. I shared his sense of accomplishment when he graduated from Stanford with a major in international relations.

From the moment I returned from Vietnam I tried to make up for my absence at Chris's birth by being there for him. I wanted him (just as I wanted my other two children) to grow up knowing beyond a shadow of a doubt that his father loved him.

I still remember the day—Chris was probably four at the time—when Margaret Ann and I were recounting for him the details of his birth. It may have been in the context of a discussion about his baby sister's arrival, I don't recall. But I'll never forget his reaction at what was evidently his first realization that I had been on the other side of the world when he'd been born and hadn't come home or been able to experience the first ten months of his life. He broke down and cried inconsolably.

I still recall feeling his sudden sadness. I can't begin to imagine the *constant* sadness Mai lives with, knowing that her father chose to leave her and never returned. She grew up never knowing a father's love, yet never willing to quit hoping that she would someday have it.

While there's little realistic hope that Mai and thousands like her will ever find their fathers, now there is at least some hope she can find a better life than what she knew growing up on the streets in Vietnam.

## Welcome Home?

Finally, in 1987, Congress passed the Amerasian Homecoming Act. That's what helped Mai come to this country.

This act established a two-year period (later extended) during which Amerasians born between January 1, 1962, and January 1, 1976, and their immediate families, could enter the United States with immigration and refugee status. Thousands (though only a small percentage of those who might have qualified) have persevered to work their way through the complicated legal and diplomatic obstacle course to immigrate to the States.

But even for many of the Amerasians who made it to the U.S., this bill may have been too little, too late. It's called a "homecoming" act. But can America ever feel like "home" to anyone who spent the first twenty-two years of her life on the streets of Saigon? There's irony and something of an indictment in the very title of this bill. "Homecoming" sounds warm and welcoming. But if we mean it now, an entire generation after we walked away from Vietnam, why didn't we bring these kids home any sooner? The road ahead for many Amerasian immigrants won't be much smoother than what they've already traveled. J. Kirk Felsman, a Dartmouth Medical School professor and an expert on Amerasian resettlement, says:

All too many of the Amerasians we are working with are poorly equipped—socially, educationally and psychologically—to make the kind of adjustment and eventual adaptation to life in America that most of us would judge to be adequate.

Without additional support to help Amerasians achieve a reasonable degree of economic and emotional self-sufficiency, many may fall into a cycle of poverty, gang membership, and welfare dependency.

Felsman argues that the Homecoming Act was

myopic, being almost exclusively focused on expediting emigration. It contained little balance of attention and virtually no fiscal
allocation to address the hard human issues of actual resettlement.
Unlike earlier waves of Vietnamese refugees, the Amerasians have
little educational background—up to fifteen per cent have no formal
education and seventy-five per cent have less than four years of
schooling. The majority are illiterate in Vietnamese and arrive in
America with no transferable job skills.

When I went back to Vietnam in 1988, and even after I met Mai
and had confronted the sad plight of the Amerasians, World Vision
had no plans to try to respond to their special needs. But then along
came a generous donor, a Vietnam vet who had since made a
fortune in business and wanted to help World Vision help the
people of Vietnam.

We told him about our relief work, the medical assistance and
the prosthetic supplies, and he donated money for those things. But
it was what we told him about Mai and the other Amerasians that
truly moved him. He said, "I lost a lot of friends who were killed
in Vietnam. And while I don't have any way of knowing if any of
those friends fathered Amerasian children, the possibility makes me
want to help those kids."

He promised a challenge grant, matching other donations dollar
for dollar up to a million dollars, for special Vietnam-related relief
projects. More than half the $2 million raised would go specifically
for an Amerasian program.

We quickly set out to determine how we could put our money
to best use. In cooperation with another evangelical Christian group,
World Relief, and other agencies, we contributed major funding for
English teachers and for recreation and family-activity facilities at
the refugee orientation center in the Philippines. And as a means
of assisting in the resettlement of Amerasians into American life, we

established one-on-one mentoring programs in cooperation with local churches in twenty-five of the American "cluster cities" where most of the Amerasians settle.

I have visited the six-month orientation camp in Bataan, Philippines, where Amerasians are taught how to flush a toilet, purchase groceries in a supermarket, use a post office and read help-wanted ads in English-language newspapers.

But perhaps the biggest challenge faced by any of the agencies, whether religious or secular, who are trying to respond to the special needs of this long-forgotten group is to somehow prepare them for the disappointment and disillusionment that must come when they finally give up on their lifelong dreams of finding their fathers.

It seemed every Amerasian I met at the orientation center had some cherished clue to show me. A single letter, a photo, perhaps a bank account record with a name. But the trail was cold. Every scrap of evidence I saw was from 1975 or before. Fewer than two per cent will ever be reunited with the father they long to meet.

The coordinator of World Vision's Amerasian program in Phoenix explained: "The father figure is very strong in Vietnamese culture. Amerasians need to find out who their father is to help them establish some sense of identity. They need the contact to give their lives credibility."

This attitude is reflected in the words of Trang Thi Thuy Lam, an Amerasian young woman now living in Arizona. "I don't know who my father is," she says. "I went to Alabama and asked a friend to help me, but we couldn't find him. The United States is very big."

She adds, "It has been twenty years already. A lot of people have fathers. Not me. I don't want him to give me money or help me. I just want to know who he is."

For kids like this, for young people like Mai who are now making the difficult adjustment to life in America, the painful hope of someday finding a father fades much more slowly than the old photos and wrinkled letters that remain their most cherished possessions. Their hope may well mark them as the most pathetic victims of the Vietnam War. They too, like the MIAs and all the Vietnam vets we've already talked about, are missing the peace we will focus on in Section III.

But first, there are still other victims of this war without closure.

# 7
# The Refugees:
# Say Hello
# to Your New
# Homeland

Not long ago, I had lunch in a Southern California restaurant with a teenage Vietnamese boy named B.J. and the Christian couple who had adopted him. Long before we met that day, I had known something of B.J.'s story.

In April 1975, as communist forces threatened to overrun Saigon, thousands upon thousands of frightened South Vietnamese tried to leave the country any way they could. Those with political connections or money expended whatever resources they had in their desperate attempts to escape.

There were many with no such resources. And in what was an admirable act of humanity, someone made arrangements to save a large group of young orphan children by flying them out of Vietnam and bringing them to America for adoption. About two hundred fifty Vietnamese youngsters were loaded onto a giant C-5 military cargo craft and sent off to a new and better life. B.J., an infant at the time, was aboard that plane.

But something happened as the mercy flight lifted off from the Tan Sun Nhut airfield. A hydraulic problem? Sabotage? No one ever knew for certain. But that big C-5, with its precious human cargo and full fuel tanks, crashed and exploded in a rice paddy not far from the end of the runway.

I vividly remember the newspaper and television accounts. Not only had these helpless kids lost their parents, they were losing their country and any chance of growing up in their own culture. And now, with one last ray of hope for survival, almost two hundred of them had lost their lives.

After all they had been put through, we couldn't even fly them out of the country safely! For me, in 1975, that crash seemed a tragically fitting symbol of the American effort in Vietnam. It seemed to sum up powerfully the failure and futility of the whole Vietnam experience.

Fortunately for B.J., his story didn't end there. When the plane slammed into that rice paddy, he was miraculously thrown clear. The natural mud pack in which his tiny body landed protected him from the flames. He was rescued and given another chance to fly out of Vietnam.

When I met him he was a healthy, happy teenager living in Fresno, California, with his adopted American family. A good-looking kid, with a 3.9 GPA, a member of his school's basketball team.

As we shared our lunch, I told B.J. about my memory of that crash and the feelings it had aroused. And I rejoiced to see such a happy ending for at least one of those children.

*　　*　　*　　*

Since Adam and Eve fled the garden, our world has had no shortage of refugees. The refugee experience provides a recurring theme throughout the Bible. Noah and his family were refugees from the great flood. Joseph's family went to Egypt to escape the famine in their own land. Four hundred years later, Moses led a refugee people across the Sinai to establish the refugee nation of Israel. Mary and Joseph, along with baby Jesus, became refugees when they fled to Egypt to escape the wrath of King Herod. And the refugee experience has continued to the present day. Every natural disaster—earthquake, hurricane, flood or famine—and every war in world history has produced its refugees.

\*　\*　\*　\*

World Vision, the organization of which I head the U.S. branch, began as a small attempt by American Christians to help refugee children from the Korean War. It has grown over the years to become a truly international partnership aimed at providing both short-term relief and longer-term development assistance to millions of suffering people around the world each year. Many of them are refugees.

We've spearheaded a wide variety of projects in response to such diverse victims as Romanian orphans with AIDS, entire villages facing starvation in famine-stricken lands such as Ethiopia and the Sudan, and those victimized by the fallout of Chernobyl. We've helped build homes for the poor along the Mississippi Delta and create jobs in inner-city Los Angeles. Yet a major focus of our work has always been the refugees of war and political conflict around the world—the Kurds in Iraq, the Cambodians escaping the killing fields, the Palestinians in the Middle East, the Afghans fleeing the fighting in their war-torn land, the Nicaraguan villagers caught in the Central American crossfire, and many other groups around the world.

And in fact, one of the most colorful chapters in World Vision's history centers on our attempt to respond to the needs of another group of victims of the war in Vietnam—a group that became known to the world as the "Boat People."

## Fleeing Vietnam

During the months, weeks and days before Saigon fell in 1975, many people left Vietnam. They were the governmental and military leadership of South Vietnam, others with strong ties to the decade-long American presence in their country, and those with the wherewithal to bargain or buy their way out. Most of them eventually resettled in America in what was to be the first big wave of Vietnamese refugees.

The second wave began in the later seventies as great numbers of Vietnamese decided the terrible, uncertain risk of an unlawful escape would be preferable to the suffering they were enduring under the Communists. Realizing they would be probably be killed, tortured or at least imprisoned if they were caught, tens of thousands of Vietnamese (men, women and children—sometimes entire extended families) packed what little they could carry and set off walking hundreds of miles over the rugged uncharted terrain of Laos or the treacherous jungles of Vietnam's neighboring enemy Cambodia, in hopes of eventually reaching the border of Thailand. A staggering number of survivors found their way over the mountains or survived the jungle without being caught in the battle between the Vietnamese and Cambodian armies to reach temporary safety in the rapidly mushrooming refugee camps along the Thai border. They told harrowing tales of hardship, determination and courage.

But the refugees who caught the attention of the watching world and symbolized the desperation and courage of the South Vietnamese people were those who tried to escape their homeland by sea. Phong Ngoc Hunyh was one of those.

On a dark June night in 1979 a small boat drifted silently downriver in the Bac Lieu province of Vietnam's delta country.

Beneath the deck of the sixty-foot boat, Phong, his twenty-five-year-old wife, Ank Ngot Tran, and their two small children huddled silently with 285 other Vietnamese and prayed their craft would reach the sea without being discovered.

Phong had been a corporal in the South Vietnamese Air Force. When the Communists took power, he became a prisoner—forced to build dikes for rice paddies. His captivity lasted only three months. But even after his "release" he was forbidden to leave his home village, his electricity and running water were turned off and he was forced to work in the rice fields for the next three and a half years.

Earlier plans to escape never worked out. But this time, after months of extensive secret planning involving sixteen different families, Phong and his family were finally making their bid for freedom. As the boat slid past the river mouth and began bobbing in the rough waters of the South China Sea, Phong wondered if he would ever see his homeland again. There was considerable doubt they would survive on the open sea in a boat built for river travel. But for Phong, even death at sea seemed preferable to what he'd been through in the past few years. Once clear of the Vietnamese coast, the boat turned south and headed for Singapore. Except for crowded conditions and seasickness, everything went fine the first day. But on the second day, a fishing boat deliberately rammed the refugee vessel and then the fishermen-turned-pirates boarded the crippled craft at gunpoint, threatening to kill everyone aboard unless they surrendered all their money and valuables. The pirates took two of Phong's wife's rings and the family watches. As they left with their loot, the pirates again rammed the small boat amidships, weakening its timbers.

At least they left without harming anyone. Such pirates boarded other refugee vessels, shot the men, repeatedly raped the women and threw children overboard to the sharks. One refugee boat was boarded, robbed and terrorized ten different times in fourteen days.

Phong's boat wasn't attacked a second time. But it was heavily damaged and leaking badly when, four days after leaving Vietnam, it ran aground near Trengganu, Malaysia. The refugees abandoned their craft and stumbled to shore, only to be met by Malaysian soldiers demanding "Gold, gold!" and then beating them—the women and children with sticks and the men with rifle butts.

All the refugees were herded into a roped-off area for the night. And after dark other Malaysians came by flashlight to demand gold, jewelry and money. They found little left to steal.

Next morning Phong and the others were moved to another beach a few miles away and placed inside a barbed-wire enclosure with five hundred other boat people who had landed earlier. For ten days they had no food other than what they had salvaged from their boat. All they had to drink was brackish water they found by digging thirty feet down into the sand.

Finally a small supply of food came from the United Nations High Commission on Refugees. And Malaysian officials announced the group was going to be transferred. A Malaysian navy ship appeared, towing five small fishing boats. Divided into five groups, the refugees were loaded aboard.

Phong and his family were among ninety-three people crammed into a thirty-foot-long, eight-foot-wide boat. Then the navy ship set out to sea, towing all five fishing boats behind at speeds up to fifteen knots, shipping a lot of water and forcing the refugees to bail frantically to stay afloat. After twenty hours of towing, the Malaysians cut the tow rope and set the crowded fishing vessels adrift on the high seas.

When the elected captain of Phong's boat shouted that he had no water and only a couple gallons of fuel, a sailor told him to shut up, fired a shot over his head and then pointed his gun at the boat. The "captain" dove to the deck and the navy ship steamed away.

The refugee boats took quick stock of their situation. The one boat with an adequate supply of fuel headed for Indonesia's Anambas Islands. The remaining four boats devised a fuel-saving plan: two boats would pull the other two for a time, and then they'd switch off. But the combination of rusty fuel and sea water seeping through the cracked engine block quickly fouled the diesel engine on Phong's boat. Rough seas soon separated the remaining boats and they began to drift helplessly.

The men tied tarps together for makeshift sails. But the winds only blew them north toward Vietnam. For the first three days they had no fresh water. The adults drank sea water and the children drank the urine of the adults. They prayed for rain. But when a squall finally provided enough water to catch and drink, it brought with it chilly winds. And there was no shelter on the crowded boat. Their only food was what little uncooked rice they'd saved from the Malaysian beach.

Twice they floated past fishing boats that refused to help. Day after day they drifted. When food and water ran out, so did their strength and hope.

**Operation Seasweep**

More than a year before, while Phong and everyone aboard that little boat were still making plans to escape Vietnam, the *Los Angeles Times* had run an article with a photo of a terrified Vietnamese refugee mother, holding her little girl as their boat was about to be pulled back out to sea after landing on the coast of Thailand. The president of World Vision at that time, the late Stan Mooneyham, was speaking one night in a Baptist church in the Watts section of Los Angeles when the pastor handed him the clipping, waited for Stan to read it, and then asked, "Well, what are you going to do about it?"

Stan didn't know what to say. To start with, he wasn't sure why anyone should expect him or World Vision to do anything. The media hadn't reported much on the problem at that time. But Stan did a little research and discovered that the number of boat people trying to escape Vietnam was rapidly increasing—to several thousand a month. Conservative estimates said half of all who tried to escape by boat died at sea.

Stan Mooneyham's first idea was that World Vision could save thousands of lives by equipping a mercy ship to pick up refugees from their crowded, unseaworthy boats. He visited a number of countries, but no government would guarantee entry or permission for any rescued refugees to resettle. Each country said it already had more refugees than it could process. All the governments acknowledged the problem: thousands of refugees were drowning at sea. But no one would give them permission to land. Even big commercial vessels were sailing past disabled refugee boats without offering to help—because of the resettlement difficulties.

The official advice of everyone, including U.S. government officials, was *do nothing*. And there seemed little that could be done. Then another World Vision executive had an idea. While no one would grant permission to rescue the refugees, no permission would be needed to launch a supply mission. World Vision could equip a ship with basic food and supplies to give to refugees and even repair boats to enable them to reach shore under their own power.

So that's what World Vision did in the summer of 1978. A 300-ton ship was bought and supplied with food, fuel, clothes, medicine and engine parts. Its crew included a medical team and mechanics to repair engines. The ship, christened the *Seasweep*, would not take on refugee passengers. But rather than leave anyone to drown in an irreparable boat, World Vision actually purchased some small, seaworthy craft to trade free-of-charge to refugees on the verge of sinking. In accordance with international regulations, the *Seasweep* crew didn't direct any boats toward a particular country. But they made sure each captain was given charts and a working compass, shown his location and allowed to choose his own course for the nearest land. Operation Seasweep was so successful, before it had to be called off at the start of the fall typhoon season, that World Vision decided to continue the project the next summer. The original ship was traded for a 1400-ton, 300-foot cargo ship that could carry more supplies, sail in stormier seas, and even had a crane rig capable of lifting refugee boats out of the water for repairs. After outfitting the ship and spending months hassling with various governments before finally getting the ship registered, the second *Seasweep* finally set sail on its maiden voyage out of Singapore on July 6, 1979—just three days after the Malaysian navy vessel had set Phong's boat adrift. The *Seasweep* headed north, looking for refugee boats, but saw nothing for the first three days.

## Rescue!

On July 8, two Thai fishing boats spotted the drifting boat carrying Phong and his family. Attaching a rope between their two boats, the fishermen passed on either side of the refugee craft and tried to capsize it.

The adult refugees prayed and frightened children cried as the rope rocked their boat. The fishermen only laughed and continued their game. Mercifully, the rope broke before it could tip the boat and the fishermen motored away.

That evening the *Seasweep* sailed close enough to the Malaysian coast near the Thai border to take a reckoning from an on-shore beacon. Then it turned northeast toward Vietnam. The next day, July 9, a lookout on the *Seasweep* spotted what looked like a drifting boat.

When Phong finally noticed the approaching ship his first thought was, *friend or foe?* But then he thought, *It doesn't matter.* He felt sure they were all going to die anyway. Few of the refugees mustered enough energy to wave. Some of them feared the big ship might be a Russian vessel which would only deliver them back to Vietnam.

Then someone saw the name *Seasweep* and began yelling, "Our savior! You're our savior!" Several of the refugees had learned about the mercy ship from a Vietnamese-language magazine which had been smuggled into the country from the United States.

Sugar water and food were quickly passed down to the deck of the small boat, and four refugees were taken aboard the *Seasweep* on a basket stretcher for emergency medical attention. The *Seasweep's* chief engineer went down to check out the small boat's engine and soon reported that it was cracked, full of sea water and would never run again. Since the *Seasweep* wasn't going to leave anyone aboard what amounted to a floating coffin, the order was given to take the refugees aboard.

It took several days of intense negotiations before government officials in Singapore finally, grudgingly, allowed the *Seasweep* to bring the refugees into port. And that only after the U.S. government guaranteed to accept them all for resettlement.

Phong and his family finally got their chance for freedom and a new life in California.

**Happy Ending?**

As incredible as Phong's ordeal was, his family's story certainly isn't unique. Thousands of Vietnamese boat people could tell similar survival tales full of suffering, danger and despair.

Perhaps one reason we find such stories so fascinating and inspiring is that they remind us of lessons too long forgotten in our protective American culture. For in the example of Phong, and tens of thousands like him, we see perseverance overcoming pain and suffering. We understand the price and the value of freedom. We're encouraged by the strength and resiliency of the human spirit.

Yet how quickly we forget those lessons when the refugee stories drop from our newspapers and TV evening news. How quickly our respect and empathy are replaced by different reactions when the refugees, be they Vietnamese or any other group, move into our neighborhoods and compete for our jobs.

The refugee experience never ends when the boat finally reaches a safe shore. Neither does it end when, after months in refugee camps, immigration papers arrive. Or even when the plane lands or the ship docks in a new country.

The inspiring saga of the Vietnamese refugees continues today. Their work ethic and their enterprising nature have enabled tens of thousands not only to adjust to life in the States but to succeed in American trade, business and education.

An impressively high number of Vietnamese children have grown up to become valedictorians in our high schools and honor graduates from our finest colleges and universities. Their accomplishments are as much a tribute to the character of the Vietnamese people as was the courage of their parents who risked everything for freedom.

But when we remember and marvel at the wonderful survival stories of the boat people and kids like B.J., when we recognize and respect their remarkable adjustment and accomplishments here in America—it's easy to forget what they have lost and are still missing.

**What Is Lost**
As Americans we're big on family values, patriotism and the American way. All of these themes were powerfully illustrated and repeatedly echoed during and after the Persian Gulf War. How many heart-rending family-related stories did the American media carry about loved ones separated by the Gulf War and then the joyous returns to home and hearth? How many speeches made mention of things like "American pride" and "national unity"? How many times did we hear military men and women stationed halfway

around the world in the middle of an Arab culture telling interviewers how they longed for sausage pizzas, soft beds and college football?

We understood those themes, because our own personal and corporate feelings for family, country and culture are such a big part of our identity as Americans.

If we understand this about ourselves, we should relate to the Vietnamese refugee experience as it continues today. Traditionally, the family, especially the extended family, plays a much bigger and more vital role in the daily life of the Vietnamese than it does in our mobile American society. For the Vietnamese, family provides not only the emotional basis for personal identity, but a practical support system offering wisdom, guidance and help for everything from career and marriage decisions to child care.

As Americans we take immense pride in our two hundred years of national history and our great democratic tradition of independence won from the British in a courageous, seven-year revolutionary war. In comparison, Vietnam's colorful national history goes back nearly *two thousand* years with a centuries-long struggle for independence from the Chinese, the Mongols and in this century the French.

We feel such attachment as Americans to our modern Western culture, so much of which has developed in the post-industrial, communication-and-computer age of the twentieth century. Much of Vietnamese culture still finds its basis in Chinese tradition, the practices and roots of which go back long before the time of Christ.

The Vietnamese refugees, for all they have survived and achieved, have lost much of their connection with their rich family, national and cultural heritage. Virtually every refugee has lost loved ones or been separated from them with little hope of re-establishing those ties. Almost none can yet return to their homeland—even for a visit. And as they strive to establish a new life for their families in a new land, they have to realize their children and grandchildren are developing a very different cultural identity.

In all these ways, the Vietnamese refugees are inspiring examples of courage and strength in the face of hardship. And they are yet another group who remain victims of an unresolved war.

# 8

## Our Former Allies . . . and the Church in Vietnam

Time and again on each trip back to postwar Vietnam, I view scenes, meet people and experience situations that prompt the recurring thought: *Vietnam may have won the war, but it is definitely losing the peace.*

Here is a country that has known little but war for forty years. It has refused to back down from and has defeated in turn France, the United States and then China. Yet two generations of "successful" warfare has produced no real winners, only losers. For just as surely as those Vietnamese refugees who escaped their homeland, the millions of people who remain in Vietnam are also victims.

I will never forget a twenty-year-old boy I met in a rehabilitation center in DaNang. He said he'd been orphaned at the age of ten. Five years ago he stepped on a land mine, left over from the war, as he was walking on the outskirts of the city. He lost both legs just below the knee. But he made sure to thank me for the money and supplies World Vision provided to the rehab clinic and for the resin used to make the prosthetic devices he hoped would enable him to walk again.

Outside the capital city another young man hit a mine while plowing a field. The explosion blew off half his face. Unfortunately, such tragedies are regular occurrences in a land still laced with unexploded bombs and mines. In the Hue region alone there are an estimated 7.5 million explosive charges waiting to go off and create more victims of a war that has been over for almost a generation.

The most reliable figures I've seen indicate there are at least 60,000 war-related amputees in Vietnam and more than two million handicapped invalids—a hugely disproportionate number in a nation of sixty-seven million. And while not all of Vietnam's handicapped population can be directly attributed to the war, the low-quality medical treatment most of them receive reflects the priorities of a government that sinks forty-five per cent of its annual gross national product into the support of its military and has virtually nothing left to spend on health care.

I held a beautiful three-year-old girl in my arms on a visit to a polio center in Ho Chi Minh City. She was just one of 10,000 polio victims in that city alone—with more cases showing up every month. In light of the government's failure to provide even minimal and inexpensive immunizations, UNICEF officials have tried to institute a basic child survival program—but there remains an appalling lack of primary health understanding, particularly in rural areas. Families are too busy working in the fields for food to bring children to clinics for immunization. Mothers don't want to see their little ones cry, so they shield them from the needle. Sterilization is practically unheard of in the countryside.

**Medical Crisis**

Those who do seek medical help find facilities terribly inadequate. The polio center I visited was one example. Founded in 1983, it was housed in an old building which had once been a barracks for South Vietnamese airborne troops. What little medical equipment the hospital contained was so old that replacement parts were no longer being made.

In my various tours of Vietnamese hospitals I found none that compared with the medical facilities available within most American university athletic departments. And those were the major city hospitals in places like Ho Chi Minh City, DaNang and Hanoi; medical resources in rural Vietnam were even worse.

The government has established a network of "commune clinics" throughout the country. But the medical staff working in these clinics often has little training and even less in the way of provisions to work with. In one clinic I visited there were only four bottles of pills for six thousand people. The medicine cabinet in the average American home is better stocked than any of the rural clinics I've visited in Vietnam. The most positive sign is that medical personnel seem as eager for additional training as they are thankful for any supplies or equipment they receive. Meantime they have to be resourceful with what they have. Natural medicines are still widely used: bark, roots, dried locust husks (a popular remedy for diarrhea) and the like.

In DaNang, I visited a poly-clinic (between a hospital and a clinic in terms of sophistication) where a mother had brought a two-year-old boy suffering from food poisoning as the result of eating diseased fish. The clinic had no medicine to induce vomiting, so the staff inserted a rubber hose down the boy's throat, all the way to his stomach, then poured water down the tube until he became so engorged he finally threw up. Three people were required to hold the struggling toddler down for what looked more like some form of medieval torture than twentieth-century medicine. But the country's medical shortages are only symptomatic of the deeper overall problem: abject poverty.

A teacher told me all his colleagues regularly come to school without eating breakfast. Two meager meals a day are all they can ever afford.

The latest reports I've seen indicate the average Vietnamese consumes a daily ration of approximately 1600 calories a day— 1400 of which come from rice. This is far less than the minimum food intake required to maintain reasonable health and meet an average person's energy needs. Clear evidence of this is easily seen in the children. You see boys and girls who look five or six only to learn they are nine or ten; that's the result of chronic malnutrition. And even though Vietnam has become a major rice exporter in recent years, for now and the immediate future it does not have sufficient food to feed its own growing population.

### A Staggering Economy

The nation's economy is as unhealthy as its people. When I returned to Vietnam in 1988, the country appeared to be in a state of serious decay. Not only were there no new homes, factories or roads—the ones which remained hadn't been maintained for twenty years. Some new construction and repair has taken place since 1988, but the infrastructure remains too weak to support a vibrant economy.

Transportation is an ongoing problem. Major bridges over the Red River between Hanoi and the major port city of Haiphong still show bomb damage from 1972 B-52 raids. City streets are passable. But travel routes into the countryside prove a continuing challenge to motorized traffic—especially to the many vintage vehicles whose ages may soon qualify them as bona fide classic cars. The national airline flies an antiquated fleet of retired Russian planes. And the transportation of choice, the only choice, for most of the country's population remains the bicycle.

In most of Vietnam running water would be a luxury. Electricity is unreliable in the biggest cities and almost nonexistent elsewhere.

The annual inflation rate in Vietnam has been as much as 500-1,000 per cent for many years. At the same time the average annual per capita income is about $150. Most government-employed workers, including doctors and nurses, work for salaries ranging from $5-15 a month and usually have to work at second or third jobs to feed their families.

Vietnam's agriculturally based economy is powered by more water buffaloes than tractors. Most of North Vietnam's industry was decentralized and relocated throughout the countryside during the war to minimize bomb damage. Much of the South's industrial base was dismantled or destroyed in the early years of "liberation." Add to that the double postwar death blow of state-run inefficiency and lack of capital, and industry cannot recover enough to produce much of anything that will sell in the international marketplace.

The economic straits of hundreds of thousands of Vietnamese families (and through them the nation's economy) are eased somewhat by millions of dollars' worth of Western goods sent into the country (much of it illegally) each year from Vietnamese friends and relatives resettled in other countries. Western-made items such as cassette recorders, replacement parts for hot plates and, of course, blue jeans are big sellers on the Vietnamese black market.

In fact, the hope of establishing their own supply line for such goods has inspired a growing number of financially desperate families to save up enough money to purchase passage for a son or a nephew on one of the refugee boats that continue to leave Vietnam's shores for Hong Kong, Singapore and other Southeast Asian ports. If just one relative survives to reach a refugee camp and eventually resettles in the West, the Western products and money he sends back to his family will significantly improve the entire clan's standard of living and may be the family's best hope for survival.

In the seventies and eighties tens of thousands of Vietnamese unwilling to risk, or perhaps unable to afford, passage on a refugee boat escaped the country temporarily in a legal manner. They applied for jobs in the Soviet Union and other Eastern-bloc countries The pay was never much by Western standards, but it gave Vietnamese workers better access to Western goods and extra money to send home for the support of their loved ones. However, the recent collapse of communist regimes in eastern Europe sent many Vietnamese packing for home where they have re-entered a work force already bloated by tens of thousands of ex-military personnel returning home from Cambodia after years of Vietnamese occupation. This greater-than-ever competition in a weak job market has come at a time when economic and political events in Russia, Vietnam's primary trade partner and benefactor, raise serious questions about that superpower's continued support. The combination of all these developments practically guarantees continued economic struggle and threatens to knock the props out from under the nation's already staggering economy.

## Friends in Need

Inadequate health care, a poverty-stricken lifestyle and a badly crippled economy impact the entire population. But within Vietnam there are certain population segments, each with its own specific experiences, that I have come to consider victims of the war's continuing lack of closure.

The first group is made up of our former South Vietnamese allies. As an American who fought to help protect these people, I can't help feeling frustration, sadness and a measure of corporate guilt for all they have endured since their "liberation." We convinced them to pick sides; we made them (as a nation and individually) dependent on us for everything from guns to butter. We asked them to stake their lives on our friendship and support . . . and then we changed our policy and abandoned them.

When the South fell to the Communists in 1975, all those who had worked with or for Americans and any others having ties to the American-backed South Vietnamese government or military were all suspect. Along with most of the South's professional people—doctors, lawyers, teachers and successful business owners, they were rounded up and marched off to what amounted to prison work camps but were euphemistically termed *trai cai tao,* which translates literally, "camp/transform/re-create."

The routine in the re-education camp consisted of backbreaking labor in rice paddies from morning to night combined with constant indoctrination in the teachings of Communism. Those who survived did so on less-than-subsistence rations and by avoiding the brutal beatings guards regularly administered to those who weren't working or learning well enough.

The luckiest of our allies were sentenced to only a few months of re-education. Many endured years of such treatment with little or no contact with family or friends. The latest reports indicate some are still being held today.

Thousands, perhaps tens of thousands, never came back from the camps. Those who did were often still considered suspect by the new communist regime. This was especially true of educated professionals, many of whom were blackballed and have found nothing but the most menial of jobs. Many now work as cyclo drivers in Ho Chi Minh City—former professional and government officials who have to pedal Western visitors around the city for pennies a day in order to feed their families.

I've talked with several of these cyclo drivers. A great number of them speak very good English and are in that way uniquely qualified for their new positions which bring them into contact with so many foreigners. Some, when they realize I'm American, are willing to talk about their experience since 1975. They don't share many of the details. But their pain and anger pour out in a shocking torrent of English swear words (we certainly taught them to swear well) when they refer to the communist government and especially their re-education-camp guards.

## A Church at Risk

Yet another group of victims are those who make up the church. There are an estimated 6.3 million Christians in Vietnam today— six million Catholics and three hundred thousand Protestants. As a Christian myself, and given my role in a Christian organization that had close ties with the Vietnamese church prior to 1975, I have a special interest and concern for my Christian brothers and sisters in Vietnam. On Sundays when we're in there, World Vision staff people make it a point to worship in one or more of the local churches. After attending a Catholic church in DaNang one Sunday morning, we met with a local Protestant pastor who invited us to a service at his church that evening. We asked if anyone would be put in jeopardy by our attendance. The pastor told us no and enthusiastically encouraged us to come.

The church was packed! I couldn't help being moved and inspired by the congregation's courage as I listened to them sing in Vietnamese the old gospel hymn "Standing on the Promises." Here they were, boldly proclaiming the Word, knowing the congregation was sprinkled with spies for the communist government. This scene was repeated in Ho Chi Minh City just three nights later when we visited an evangelical church where 250 believers showed up for a midweek Bible study and prayer service.

The Christian church in Vietnam today evidences surprising vitality. But its steely strength has come at great price, tempered by long years of hardship and persecution.

Officially, Vietnam's constitution promises everyone freedom of religion. No one is to be coerced into participating in any religious activities or prevented from worshiping as he or she chooses. Church buildings are to be protected by the state. And religious groups are to be permitted to establish their own training schools.

But of course all religious activities are subject to very specific government rules and restrictions, the enforcement of which is left to the discretion of local communist officials. That means religious restrictions can vary greatly from region to region and province to province.

Most priests and pastors in South Vietnam were automatically shipped off to re-education camps in 1975. A number of them weren't released for more than a decade.

The present church leaders face continued hardship and restrictions. Many may not journey outside their home provinces. The government refuses to allow denominational or national meetings for the purpose of organizing or electing church leadership. The families of ministers are often denied educational opportunities, and I've heard accounts of pastors whose children were refused medical treatment at government hospitals and clinics.

### One Brave Man

Individual Christians also pay a price for their faith. One of the most inspiring people I've met in Vietnam is a very distinguished middle-aged university professor. He told me his story. He received an American higher education, which included study at a small Christian college in the southeastern U.S. He returned home to South Vietnam after completing his graduate work in 1974, just months before the country fell to the Communists.

Somehow he avoided being exiled to a re-education camp. But he was forced to spend the next two years in an intensive study of

Marxism and Leninism. Even after he successfully completed his socialist indoctrination program, he searched long and hard before landing a temporary position teaching in a government university in Saigon. While he was finally allowed to do what he had trained to do—which was teach—he lived with constant uncertainty because the school would give him nothing more than a day-to-day contract.

He told me, "I tried to be a good Marxist and believe communism was the way. But after a couple years I realized in my own heart I had to believe in Jesus and return to the church." When the school administration learned he was attending a Christian church, they offered him a difficult choice.

He could attend church or he could teach.

He chose to teach and support his family and to continue to worship God on his own.

"It was so easy for me to be a Christian in America," he told me. "Much harder here. Everyone goes to church in the United States. Here being a Christian is very lonely for me. I must be careful who I talk to. So I pray and spend much time studying the Word of God."

He smiled. "I'm much stronger Christian now. Much closer to God now than in the United States."

Some years ago he found another teaching position at a new university where he is now a permanent and respected member of the faculty. I asked if the administration at this school knows of his faith.

He nodded emphatically. "Oh yes! It is no secret. I remember a Christian teacher in America who once told me, 'Honesty is always the best policy.' He was right. I don't want to deceive anyone. I don't talk about God in my classes, but people know what I believe. When I was appointed a permanent member of the faculty, the president of our university said, 'He's a Christian but that's okay. He doesn't drink or smoke or lie or steal. He's an honest man. We should hire him.' "

My professor friend told me he still is not allowed to worship with other Christians, but he believes if he works hard, continuing to prove his integrity and his value to the university, that will change. "Very soon now," he said, "I will go and ask permission to attend church again."

In the meantime, he insisted he is content with his lot. After all, he is teaching young people. And he earns almost $300 a year—enough to provide his family with a home and to pay for a motor scooter to travel to and from the university. He insists he'd rather be where he is today than anywhere else in the world.

As we concluded our long conversation he made a memorable statement that for me summed up his inspiring faith. He said, "I have learned much about God. And I do not believe he has thrown me into this ocean to drown me, but to cleanse me. And someday he will help me to climb out"—he grinned—"maybe with a fish in my mouth."

Every time I go back to Vietnam, more and more people come up and identify themselves as Christians. I remember one student at a college I visited. When I was introduced to his class I told the group I was with World Vision, an international Christian relief and development agency, and I was there to see how we might help the Vietnamese people. Immediately this diminutive young man rushed to the front of the room and reached up to shake my hand. And he held on as he smiled and told me, in Vietnamese, in front of all his classmates: "I hope to meet you again. But if I don't see you again here on earth I know I will see you in the kingdom of heaven."

There seem to be thousands of such courageous Christians in Vietnam, honestly witnessing to their own faith and looking forward to the day, if not in this life then in the next, when they will be able to freely worship and fellowship with other believers. In the meantime, Vietnamese Christians remain victims of a war that ended in 1975 but has yet to be brought to closure.

\*   \*   \*   \*

Given the past and present circumstances, our former South Vietnamese allies and the Christians of Vietnam are two groups we might not be surprised to find among the war's victims. But I have to acknowledge at least two other groups who, though we may not notice it, are victims as well.

*October 1967: Bob Seiple (left) with brother Bill during their brief overlap in DaNang*

*Bob in his new Sopworth Camel*

*"I used to fly in this one!" An A-6 after a Vietcong rocket attack*

*January 1968: Testing an offset bombing device, the day before the start of the Tet offensive*

*Vietnam today*

*Children of the Boat People, held at a detention center in Hong Kong*

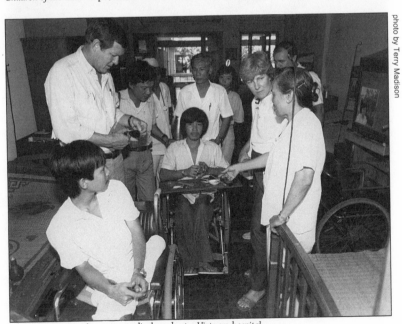

*World Vision team discussing medical needs at a Vietnam hospital*

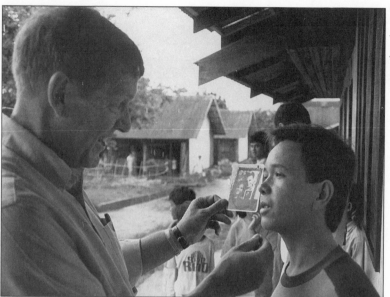

*The Amerasian boy who carried a photo of his father in hopes of someday finding him*

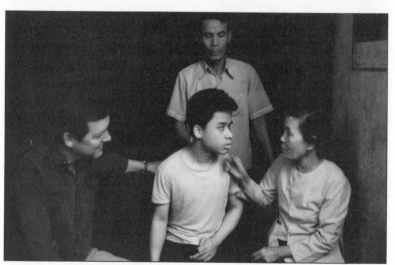

*The blind and retarded boy who sang a sweet Easter song*

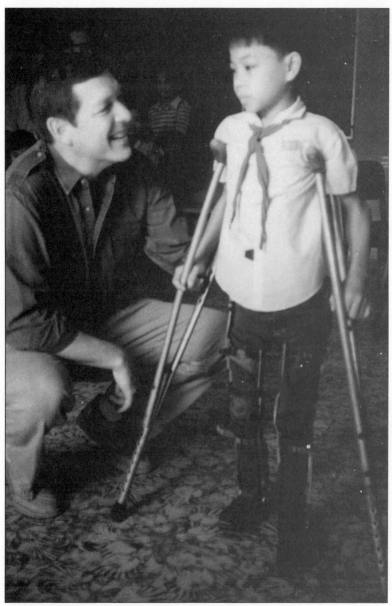

*Seeing World Vision's gifts at work—and the courage of a small boy*

*1989: Bob with Amerasians at the Bataan refugee camp in the Philippines*

*The Asian and Amerasian faces of Vietnam*

*Bob with Marine son Chris, born during Bob's first months in Vietnam as a Marine in 1968*

*Bob finds his best friend's name on the Vietnam Wall in Washington, DC*

*1988: Shaking hands with the deputy minister of labor in Ho Chi Minh City*

# 9
# The Vietcong Are People Too

I have to mention a family I met in DaNang. An elderly Vietnamese widow and her son told me their family story before she served me tea.

The woman remembers a day in 1967 when South Vietnamese soldiers came to her family's village. Her husband, a member of the Vietcong, tried to hide in a trench. "But," she said, "a traitor pointed him out and the soldiers found him and killed him." She offered no more details about what was obviously a painful memory.

But her son, sitting beside her, went on to say he'd lost a brother as well as his father in the war. He told us his brother had been a wonderful person, a bright student who spoke French well and planned to go to medical school before he joined the Vietcong— meaning he would have been this poor family's best hope for economic improvement. But he too died in the war, the family didn't know exactly when or how.

The younger son, sharing tea with us, admitted that he too had been a member of the Vietcong. But he quickly assured me he felt no bitterness or anger toward Americans or toward me as a former American soldier:

"In war time we defend our country. During war it is normal that we try to kill each other. I am told to shoot at Americans, so I shoot. But war is over now. Now we are at peace and we consider Americans our friends."

This man and his mother tell me they don't spend a lot of time thinking about the past—or about the future. There are too many things for them to worry about today. The son says he supports his mother and eleven other members of his family by transporting people on his bicycle.

This family, like other Vietcong and their supporters, may have been on the winning side of the war. But one look around the two-room shanty this widow and her family live in indicates they didn't win much. And many Vietcong remain among the war's biggest losers.

I've personally experienced the terror of a VC mortar attack. I realize the terrible toll of American lives lost to the Vietcong's guerilla warfare. I've heard stories of Vietcong brutality. I'm not, and never have been, sympathetic to their cause or their tactics.

But when you put real faces on your enemies you have to see them in a new light. I watched the deep sadness in the eyes of an old woman remembering the death of her husband and a son. I listened to the voice of an earnest, smiling man, who might well have been the one who fired rockets onto our air base in DaNang, as he talked about his struggle to support his wife, six children, his mother and an extended family. And I'll never be able to think about the Vietcong in quite the same way again.

## Terrorists or Freedom Fighters?

Not long ago I read a thought-provoking book that gave me a fresh perspective on the Vietcong. *A Vietcong Memoir: An Inside Account of the Vietnam War and Its Aftermath* (Vintage Press, 1986) was written by Truong Nhu Tang, a founder of the National Liberation Front and Minister of Justice in the Vietcong's Provisional Revolutionary Government (PRG). Truong tells of living a double, sometimes triple, life in Saigon where he served as a high official in the South Vietnamese government while at the same time working as an urban organizer for the revolution. After his capture and torture by the South Vietnamese police in 1968 he was traded in a secret U.S.-Vietcong prisoner exchange and spent the remainder of the war in the resistance jungle strongholds along the Cambodian border.

As I read Truong's account of the war, I couldn't help but notice a parallel between his story and accounts I've read in American history. In many ways similar to American revolutionaries, the Vietcong were primarily patriots. They may well have had the purest motives of any participants in the war.

The North Vietnamese Communists, despite their proclaimed goal of a unified nation of Vietnam, were invaders intending to impose their will on the South by force. Americans, despite the lofty goal of defending Southeast Asia from Communism, adopted an end-justifies-the-means philosophy to prop up and protect an inefficient, unpopular, repressive and corrupt South Vietnamese government.

The Vietcong, while throwing their lot in with the North Vietnamese Communists, were first and foremost nationalists. Many of them had fought the French in an attempt to win the freedom to establish their own representative government. But they considered the resulting Diem and Thieu regimes to be just as despotic, the country just as divided and continued foreign influence (American

*115*

instead of French) just as troubling.

So the Vietcong, like our own American revolutionaries, fought a war of resistance against the world's most powerful nation. And like our American forefathers, this band of rag-tag revolutionaries, capitalizing on a home-field advantage, perseverance and unconventional warfare, did the unthinkable. They won. They sent the world's number one superpower packing for home. But that's as far as the parallel goes, as *A Vietcong Memoir* so poignantly illustrates.

You can't read Truong's book without admiring the courage and determination it took for him to fight for his convictions. You sense and appreciate his love for his country. You have to respect the sacrifices he made for his beliefs—a well-to-do, educated, privileged leader in Vietnamese culture who left home, wife, children and parents to endure years of sickness, hardship, exile and primitive jungle living. So you can understand the incredible sense of euphoria he describes when he knows victory is finally at hand.

However, the most moving aspect of *A Vietcong Memoir* for me was reading Truong's account of victory's aftermath in the spring of 1975. Within two weeks after the fall of Saigon, Truong realized that the unity, freedom and self-determination for which he had risked everything weren't going to happen after all. He writes of the North Vietnamese Communists:

> Now with total power in their hands, they began to show their cards in the most brutal fashion. They made it understood that the Vietnam of the future would be a single monolithic bloc, collectivist and totalitarian, in which all the traditions and culture of the South would be ground and molded by the political regime of the conquerors. . . . After the 1975 victory, the Front and the PRG not only had no further role to play; they became a positive obstacle to the rapid consolidation of power.

He writes of a final meeting he called a "funeral celebration" for the top Vietcong leaders.

. . . there was no way to swallow the gall in our mouths or to shrug off the shroud that had settled on our souls. We knew finally that we had been well and truly sold.

Truong says that he and other Vietcong leaders who had spent much of their adult lives alienated from home and family wanted an end to the suffering and called for a policy of forgiveness and healing. Instead, the first year of "liberation" saw more than 300,000 South Vietnamese arrested by the Communists and shipped off to re-education camps.

Truong summarizes his own disillusionment and sorrow when he says that the South Vietnamese people

had seen the great moment finally arrive—Peace—after thirty years of continuous violence and a hundred years of hated foreign domination. But peace, which they had so passionately desired, had brought with it not blessings, but a new and even more insidious warfare, this time a warfare practiced by the liberators against their own people.

Three years of peace did something a lifetime of war hadn't been able to do. It destroyed all hope Truong Nhu Tang had for his country. In August 1978 he purchased passage on a refugee boat and fled the country with his family. He is spending the remainder of his life in exile in France—living proof that there were no "winners" in Vietnam.

### Not Even in the North

If anyone should have been a winner, it's the North Vietnamese. But all the evidence I've encountered on my trips into the North says to me these "winners" have lost at least as much as the other victims of the war.

Like their southern countrymen, the North Vietnamese suffer all the same economic hardships we talked about in the last chapter. If there's any difference at all, their experience may be even more hopeless because northern families don't have as many relatives and contacts through whom to acquire Western goods. The black market isn't as sophisticated as it is in the South and the people tend not to be as entrepreneurial. And the North Vietnamese people, only a minority of whom are active in the communist party, have every reason to be as disillusioned with the results of the war as the Vietcong. A pointed example is the story I heard of a retired North Vietnamese general, a national hero, whose elderly wife has to sell cigarettes on the street to supplement his insufficient pension; she walks two miles from their apartment every day so they won't lose face with their neighbors.

Most North Vietnamese had spent an entire lifetime enduring deprivations required by their nation's war efforts—first against the French, then against the Americans. Now they finally have peace but none of the prosperity they dreamed would be their reward for victory. They experience a malaise much like that of the Vietcong man I met in DaNang; they have little time or reason to think much about the future, because it seems almost more than they can do just to survive today. As a nation they took a chance, bet all they had on a long shot, and won. Then they discovered their victory was hollow—and they have nothing left with which to fill it.

**Loss Knows No Borders**
As much as the Vietnamese—North and South, old allies and old enemies—have lost, Vietnam doesn't hold a monopoly on the suffering resulting directly or indirectly from the Vietnam War.

Approximately 3.5 million people live in Laos, eighty per cent of them in rural areas, and many of those in the vast uncharted northern part of the country. I got my first close-up exposure to that part of the world on a recent trip to Southeast Asia.

It was supposed to be a quick side trip into rugged northern Laos. But the weather changed our plans and a premature monsoon held us hostage for twenty-four hours.

Altogether there were twenty-four of us, sharing space with some caged chickens, a small deer and a few months' supply of water-buffalo meat. We were sitting expectantly around the giant internal fuel tank of a vintage Soviet helicopter. The meat belonged to the pilot and provided considerable inspiration for him to take off as soon as the weather looked even marginal. Blood was draining from the meat and pooling on the floor in the back of the aircraft. A few more hours of tropical temperature and the meat would be rotten.

Until recently, there were no maps drawn for this part of the world. High, rugged mountains, usually shrouded in mist, with the near-constant threat of rain, provided a navigational challenge for the most experienced pilot.

We had come to visit the little town of Sam Nyer, just over the border from Vietnam, a village that had achieved critical importance during the war. Sam Nyer sat atop the Ho Chi Minh trail, the Communists' major supply link to the South. So for years this village had great value to the logisticians in the North and South. Sam Nyer was important because the trail that went through it was important.

The people who lived in the region, the Communist Pathet Lao in the valley and Hmong tribespeople in the hills, were never crucial to the war effort. It mattered to no one outside the village if every home was destroyed by American bombers; it was the land and the trail running through it that mattered.

So by the time the war ended, the people of Sam Nyer who started with little had even less. They may have been part of the "winning" side, but suddenly not even their land had value anymore. Laos became the epitome of that old cliché, "the land that time forgot." It remained difficult to reach, inaccessible to health and human services, and once again largely ignored by the rest of the world.

The people would have to be considered the poorest of the poor. Subsistence farmers try to eke out their existence on tiny plots of land. A primary farming technique is "slash and burn," a tactic that produces quick returns but is extremely shortsighted in terms of its damage to the soil. Within a couple of years the soil is useless and the lack of a root system allows massive erosion on the steep hillsides.

The difficult lot of these gentle Laotian people was in evidence when we made a trip to the local town marketplace. All some folks had to sell were long strings of frogs, alive and kicking, skewered on a sliver of bamboo. One woman's entire sales inventory consisted of a single dead rat. When we left the market, the rat had still not been sold.

Flying into Laos my thoughts had been consumed by memories of my good friend Jim. It was somewhere in these mountains or jungles where his plane went down in December 1968.

When the weather finally cleared and we flew out of the country, I thought about all the lost people of this remote land. They are indeed a people out of step with the world and falling further and further behind each year. A small, forgettable nation in a part of the world America has spent a generation trying to forget, Laos and its people remain victims of a war without closure.

### Then Came Cambodia

But the suffering in Laos can't even begin to compare with the human holocaust that took place in Cambodia after the United States pulled out of Vietnam. The American government was far more interested in re-establishing diplomatic ties with China in the late seventies than in the war being fought between Vietnam and Cambodia—a bitter regional enmity that goes back nearly two thousand years. China, which was to get its own nose bloodied in its ill-fated invasion of Vietnam from the North in 1979, backed the Khmer Rouge and its leader, Pol Pot. And while the U.S. didn't officially take sides, our government didn't mind seeing anyone oppose our old enemies, the communist Vietnamese.

For most Americans, who were trying hard not to think about Southeast Asia at all, it wasn't until 1984 and the Academy Award-winning movie *The Killing Fields* that we began to understand the extent of Cambodia's horror. It was only then we finally realized that Pol Pot and the Khmer Rouge, the allies of our new friend China, had systematically annihilated more than two million people, at one point clubbing their victims to death so as to save bullets.

The millions who died, and the traumatized nation of Cambodians who survived the atrocities of the Khmer Rouge, may be only indirectly connected to the American involvement in the Vietnam War. But the bloodbath in Cambodia, like many other developments in Southeast Asia over the last thirty years, was clearly impacted by U.S. policy. *And until there is some final closure to the war there will continue to be victims of the war throughout the entire region.*

**Welcome Back**

Given America's involvement (and my own) in the war, and given the American foreign policy which has effectively blocked Vietnam's full participation in the world community of nations ever since the war ended, I went back to Vietnam in 1988 wondering what kind of reception I would find. But on that trip, and every time I've returned since, I've been amazed at the genuine warmth shown me by the Vietnamese people—North and South.

Almost everyone asks if I've been to Vietnam before. I make it a point to be open about my role during the war; not once has that information elicited any animosity or even tempered the warmth of my reception.

Even when I'm just walking along the streets and not part of any official delegation, crowds of Vietnamese gather around when they discover I'm from the United States. And invariably several will attempt to converse with me in English.

It seems everyone wants to learn English. One of the great ironies I witnessed in Vietnam was a Soviet professor in a Vietnamese university teaching students English.

The government may not be too happy about this. But the people are making their point. Despite the long alliance between Moscow and Hanoi and the major role the former USSR played in recent Vietnamese history, the common folk want nothing to do with the Russians. But they have a great curiosity and affection for Americans. Perhaps it's because the people see their future, as well as their past, as inextricably linked to America and the West. Whatever the motive, it's as if there's a love affair between the Vietnamese and Americans.

From their side, it has so far looked pretty much like a case of unrequited love. Where Vietnamese are so quick to declare and demonstrate a love of Americans, the American public has spent most of the last sixteen years trying to forget Vietnam by relegating our public memory of the war to our corporate subconscious. And once a year, every year since 1975, our Congress has voted to continue a diplomatic and trade embargo against Vietnam.

While by itself such an embargo might not mean much, the U.S. has in effect pressured the World Bank and the International Monetary Fund to go along with the economic boycott. As a result, Vietnam has been unable to obtain the massive infusion of foreign capital needed to stimulate the economy, rebuild the nation's infrastructure and begin to alleviate the suffering of the common people.

I've already stated my thoughts on American involvement in the Vietnam War. Whether or not anyone feels the war was right, given the circumstances of the day it was understandable and perhaps even inevitable.

Ongoing debates as to whether or not our war policy was right or justifiable—like hypothetical discussions about military strategies that might have succeeded—no longer matter to the remaining victims of the war. But, however we feel about the war, *no one can feel good about the peace.* The moral issue we should all agree on concerns the years since the war ended in 1975.

Our attempts to maintain our influence in the region by imposing economic pressure have done nothing to help or heal the wounds of the region. The Vietnamese government and its communist leaders are as firmly in control as ever. It's the common people who suffer because of our policies. The innocent victims of war have now become the innocent victims of peace.

## Profile in Courage

One of the most memorable faces I've seen belongs to Lai, a nineteen-year-old Vietnamese boy I met at a small rehabilitation center World Vision helps support in DaNang.

I never learned the details of the accident, but Lai had recently been run over by a train. His right arm was severed just below the shoulder, his left arm a few inches below the elbow. He also lost his right leg well above the knee.

Lai lived in a rural province, I don't even want to *think* about how primitive was the emergency treatment he received after the accident. His stubs were sewn up but still hadn't healed properly when family and friends brought him to the rehabilitation center in DaNang, one of only ten such facilities in all of Vietnam.

He'd been at the hospital for just three days when we visited. But the staff had already fitted him with a prosthetic leg, held on with a maze of velcro-connected straps around his torso and over his shoulders.

We watched in admiration as this determined young man walked back and forth, back and forth between a set of parallel bars—trying to get a sense of balance as he learned to walk all over again. But even more amazing than his walking progress was what happened when his exercise session came to a close. Using the stub of one arm and a series of body contortions that would have shamed Houdini, Lai unfastened his harness, slipped off his artificial leg, and while balancing on his one healthy limb, carefully hung the contraption over the parallel bar before easing himself down onto a chair—exhausted.

Those of us in the therapy room broke into spontaneous applause. And he responded with a tired but proud smile. In just seventy-two hours this brave boy had gained more than the beginning of mobility. He'd found hope—not just that he would be able to walk again and that he would be fitted with artificial arms in the weeks and months ahead, but that he might do more than just survive. He might one day be able to contribute something to society. And with that hope he had begun to rediscover a sense of personal worth and dignity. I could sense that in his smiling countenance and the pride I read in his eyes.

But also on his face, between the smile and the eyes, was a painfully pathetic reminder of his current limitations. For hanging from one of his nostrils was an enormous, ugly glob of mucus. Despite his inspiring courage, despite his incredible self-determination and his newfound sense of hope for the future, Lai still had no hands with which to wipe his own runny nose.

For me, Lai symbolizes the plight of Vietnam today. It's a land full of suffering people who have known great pain, who are plodding valiantly forward, displaying courage and dignity, but still without the wherewithal to care for its own most basic human needs.

It's a land very much like Lai, a badly crippled victim desperately in need of hope—a hope that may never be found until there is healing of old wounds and true closure for the Vietnam War.

# 10
## The Names
## on the
## Wall

I t isn't as if we haven't tried to put the Vietnam War behind us. We've attempted a variety of remedies.

For years Americans practiced a national psychological defense mechanism, blocking out the memories of Vietnam by ignoring the pain and relegating all those troublesome Vietnam-related feelings to the public subconscious. But then came the delayed symptoms of post-Vietnam stress syndrome and the alarming rates of divorce, chemical dependency and suicide among Vietnam vets. All of this, along with continuing headlines highlighting Southeast Asia, eventually showed us the folly of simply pretending to forget.

**Beginning to Remember**
In the eighties America began to face the memories of Vietnam. A

wave of Vietnam-related books hit the bookstore shelves; many made the best-seller lists. Experts analyzed the war from every angle; vets wrote poignant accounts of their experiences and their emotions. Hollywood jumped on the bandwagon with follow-up movies like *Platoon, Full Metal Jacket* and *Born on the Fourth of July*. And by the end of the decade even television regularly focused on Vietnam in weekly network series such as "Tour of Duty" and "China Beach." Perhaps in response to the public's new willingness to think about Vietnam, vets around the country organized and marched in belated "Welcome Home" parades.

Many pundits noted all these trends and declared them healthy. They were seen as indication that "America is finally coming to grips with Vietnam." Of course, some of those same editorial writers and columnists argued that America's two successful military actions during the eighties—in Grenada and Panama—were at least in part a response to the American need for a military victory. Such a victory would allow the country, or at least the armed forces, to regain a sense of pride that hadn't been felt since our nation's first-ever defeat in Vietnam.

Does anyone think the developments of the eighties—in publishing, entertainment, invasions—closed the books on the specter of Vietnam? They certainly weren't paying much attention before, during or after the war in the Persian Gulf. More about the lessons of Vietnam as they relate to the Gulf War at the end of this book.

How often was the Gulf crisis compared to or contrasted with Vietnam during the days of debate before the attack on Iraq? How frequently during the war did observers and participants mention the differences between Vietnam and the Gulf in terms of everything from military strategy to press coverage to public opinion at home? And then, as soon as the cease-fire took effect, so many columnists and political cartoonists portrayed American military success against Iraq as a final exorcism of the "ghost of Vietnam." Not since the unveiling of the Vietnam War Memorial in Washington, D.C., had the op-ed pages of America's newspapers been so full of speculation that *maybe now we can begin to put the Vietnam War behind us—maybe now we can find closure.*

## The Wall

It wasn't until five years after its dedication that I first visited "The Wall." I suppose my reluctance stemmed from my first reaction when the Vietnam War Memorial was unveiled back in 1982.

I remember being all alone in a hotel room in Williamsburg, Virginia, the day after Brown had beaten William and Mary in a football game. As I watched the dedication of the Vietnam War Memorial on television, I began to cry. And I couldn't control the tears. I couldn't understand them, but I couldn't control them either.

And since I had no desire to break down like that in public, I chose not to visit the memorial in person. Until May of 1987.

Margaret Ann made the trip with me. I remained leery of my reactions, wary of some emotional ambush or deep psychological reaction that might sneak up and overcome me by surprise. But it didn't happen.

Quite frankly, when I saw the memorial up close for the first time, I felt disappointed. I was let down. It just didn't "do it" for me. I hadn't known what kind of emotion to expect, but I had expected something. However, I found nothing emotionally satisfying there.

I think I understood what the artist had attempted to do. I had followed in the media the controversy over the design during the planning of the memorial. But I'd formed no personal opinion regarding the political and aesthetic skirmishes fought over the original proposal. And I'd felt no need to take sides. I've read and appreciated the words of Maya Ying Lin, the architecture student whose design was selected in the competition held by the Vietnam

Veterans Memorial Fund committee:

> I felt the memorial should be honest about the reality of war and be for the people who gave their lives. . . . I didn't want a static object that people would just look at, but something they could relate to as on a journey, or passage that would bring each to his own conclusion. . . . I had an impulse to cut open the earth . . . an initial violence that in time would heal. . . . It was as if the black-brown earth were polished and made into an interface between the sunny world and the quiet dark world beyond, that we can't enter. . . . The names would become the memorial. There was no need to embellish.

I understood that the memorial was supposed to be an architectural statement as well as an artistic one. I had no problem with that. And yet, what I saw was simply a three-inch-thick retaining wall with nearly sixty thousand names carved on it.

Others experienced very different reactions from mine that spring day. I watched other men my age, once brothers-in-arms, some wearing faded and ill-fitting jungle fatigues, weeping before a wall of black granite mined in India and polished to a remarkable sheen that reflects, along with the sky above and the earth below, the faces and the feelings of those who stand before it.

I read the inscription:

> In honor of the men and women of the Armed Forces of the United States who served in the Vietnam War. The names of those who gave their lives and of those who remain missing are inscribed in the order they were taken from us.

But as I walked along the walls, nearly 500 feet long, 140 panels of granite in all, I was left with a dissatisfied, hollow feeling.

I believe the designer achieved her stated intent. The names are the memorial. Fifty-eight thousand, one hundred thirty-two names, arranged chronologically "in the order they were taken from us" and etched into stone. Every American known to be killed in action has a diamond inscribed next to his name. Those still missing have a cross next to theirs.

Jim Fickler's name was there. The directory said: EDWIN J. FICKLER, PANEL 34 EAST, LINE 23. I found his name high on panel 34 east. And a cross after it.

No doubt that accounted for some of my reaction that day. It struck me as both tragic and ironic that, twenty years later, the carefully planned precision of an etched marble memorial was diluted by the uncertainty regarding those still missing. Names that needed to be there if we were to err on the side of probability. *The ongoing missing are permanently recorded.* How fitting for a war without closure.

But another reason I found the memorial unsatisfying was the realization that despite the military's obsession with "body counts" in Vietnam, the war was much more than KIAs and MIAs. More than a name—your loved one, your friend—identified by its panel number, east or west, and the number of lines down from the top.

The living aren't mentioned, although so many of them were also casualties. Of the 1.3 million Americans who saw combat, nearly 300,000 were wounded, 75,000 disabled by their wounds. And then there were the loved ones scarred.

A lost war and innocence lost, replaced with cynicism—a cynicism created and shaped by the harsh realities of an imperfect world. The casualties of individuals rendered psychologically naked and defenseless. Civilian casualties, non-combative innocents, those unfortunates who found themselves in the wrong place at the wrong time. The emotional cripples of a generation. So many kinds of victims.

Their names will never be inscribed in black marble. Great panels cannot measure the ongoing price they pay. They cannot be remembered in that way . . . so they are too easily forgotten altogether.

For a time, I often thought about the movie *Platoon* in comparison to the war memorial. Where the movie attempts to say it all in two hours, the memorial attempts to say it all in sixty thousand names. The first tries to say too much, the second (in my opinion) says too little. Neither is able to capture the reality of the event.

### A Living War Memorial

My initial dissatisfaction with the Vietnam War Memorial was underscored soon after that 1987 visit. For it was on my very first trip overseas as president of World Vision, U.S., that I witnessed another kind of war memorial. Though the two had very different manifestations, I couldn't help comparing them.

The second one was actually a refugee feeding center at Peshawar, Pakistan. But there was also, in a very real way, a memorial made visible every day at this milk distribution station near the Afghanistan border.

Here, too, there were panels—panels of children. One hundred children in each line. Many lines of children seated, etched into the hard scrabble of the Afghan border lands. Panels molded out of refugees from a different war—primarily women and children.

But it's the children you see. The women in this Muslim culture remain hidden. The fathers, if they are still living, are off fighting the war. It's the children who bear youthful testimony to the horrors of war at this memorial. The children represent the visible vouchers of war, human chits, as families are allotted one liter of milk for every child at the feeding station.

Here too I noticed the reflections: the sun above shone off every imaginable type of vessel, as the panels of children gathered, row after row, in the early hours of the morning. This monument to war is organic, barely. There is still life here, the names move, the panels come and go. The living dimension of this memorial conveys a terrible reality about war's consequences that can never be communicated through marble or bronze, nor on panels or plaques.

**The Value of the Wall**
I don't want to be too hard on the Vietnam War Memorial. For no man-made monument—whether a building, a statue or a wall—can ever adequately capture the human cost of any war. No one expects it to. And the truth is, my own perspective on the memorial has changed as time's worn on.

The memorial's emotional impact hit home for me personally a couple of years ago when my son Chris gave me as a Christmas present a book called *The Wall*. It's a beautiful book of pictures, shot in photo-journalistic style, attempting to capture the essence of the Vietnam War Memorial and the reactions it elicits from those who visit. I found the book artistically powerful, but what moved me even more than the pictures were the words my son, born while I was in Vietnam, inscribed to me in the front. He wrote:

17 DEC 87
Father: I saw this book today.
I was wearing your flight jacket.
I turned the pages, I read the words, and I felt the pictures.
And there in the bookstore, with my unshaven face and my high-
    top sneakers,
I had to stop.

As my tears retreated, I marveled that a force so powerful, so deep within, could be so quickly summoned . . . I love you Dad.

Very respectfully, Chris

I recognize the psychological impact the monument has for so many of the millions of people who come to see it each year. The photos in *The Wall* capture a wide range of emotions. It is proved too by the thousands of artifacts and letters left at the base of the wall by visitors; they've all been collected and are kept in a climate-controlled warehouse in Lanham, Maryland, in what amounts to a memorial to the memorial. Given all this, I've come to appreciate the memorial for allowing such honest expressions of emotion and pain from those veterans, families and friends who come to weep unashamedly before the wall. The opportunity offered by the memorial, for Americans to admit and express their deepest emotions about the war, is as important and necessary as it was belated.

It has been an important step for the country. A first step. But it has not brought complete healing or closure to the war.

### No Wall in Vietnam

America lost 58,000. Yet more than 600,000 South Vietnamese died. The best estimates indicate the North lost over 1,000,000. So I find it interesting that Vietnam doesn't have a comparable war memorial.

Perhaps that's because there remain so many reminders of the war in Vietnam. Like the panels of Afghan refugee children, the Vietnamese victims of the war also serve as living memorials. And yet, I'm struck by the overgrown and neglected state of South Vietnam's military graveyards; it's a telling commentary in a culture that usually reveres its dead and hallows their burial places. And what about the untold thousands who died without a grave in the jungle or in some corner of a re-education-camp rice paddy? Maybe Vietnam could use a memorial.

I saw one unofficial memorial of sorts in the Philippines. I stood on a lonely stretch of beach on the coast of Bataan amidst the rusting, rotting hulls of a few tiny vessels. These boats, once the last hope of desperate families, now sit abandoned on the sand, paying silent tribute to the courage of the boat people they carried to safety and the memory of thousands of others who perished at sea.

I saw a very different "memorial" in Hanoi. And I heard part of its story from a North Vietnamese man named Louang Tan.

*　*　*　*

In December 1972, the city of Hanoi came under what was (until the Persian Gulf War) the most intense aerial bombardment in the history of modern warfare. Wave after wave, the B-52s discharged their deadly cargoes of bombs on a terrified city. The Paris Peace Talks had ruptured, and the thinking was that only a show of force would demonstrate our resolve to get our prisoners home.

That was Nixon's Christmas bombing, a horrible punctuation mark to a most difficult chapter in American history. But within a month our prisoners were home, the war for us was finally over and the nation intentionally began to turn its collective conscience away from Indochina.

When America pulled out of Vietnam, Louang Tan remained. Though for a time he wasn't sure he would survive.

When the first bombs fell that December, Tan ran to a cave hollowed out beneath his home. He stayed there frozen in fear, until the eleventh day of the bombing when a B-52 crashed right outside his home.

A quiet, reflective man, now seventy-six years old, Louang Tan calmly told his story as we stood looking at the twisted wreckage of that aircraft he told us came down on December 27, 1972. Listening to Tan reminisce on a spring day in 1990, I studied the tail section of the bomber which still juts out of a watercress pool, surrounded by simple homes in the heart of Hanoi. A woman in a tiny black-pitch boat tends the watercress around the wreckage. Children spin wooden tops in the street nearby, and girls in black pajamas wash clothes at a spigot.

Listening to Tan, and looking around, it's obvious the end of our war wasn't the end of his.

"There were many innocent civilians killed," he remembers. "We experienced much pain. We must relieve the pain of the victims." I noticed how he fused the present with the past as he talked about the impact of the war on both sides. "The war was meaningless. It only created victims. Innocent people are the victims, both American and Vietnamese. Vietnamese people are just like American people. We all suffer because of war."

Louang Tan went on to encourage us not to remain silent. "The innocent people continue to cry out," he said. "And there are more than we realize."

Hearing those words I thought of the many faces of the victims I'd seen—in Vietnam and back home in America. As I stood looking at the wreck of an airplane that remains an impromptu memorial— a striking and effective reminder of the war for the people of Hanoi, I thought of all the tears shed before the Wall. Men weeping for something they could not articulate in any other way. I thought also about the incredible sadness of innocence forever lost, and of the deep and lasting pain that has yet to be reconciled.

"Yes," I agreed with my new friend Tan, "there are more victims than we realize."

### Searching for Closure

Looking back over the past couple of decades, it seems that America as a nation and many of us as individuals have had an almost schizophrenic reaction to Vietnam. We can't bear to remember it, but we can't manage to forget it. We want to remember the dead, but we'd rather forget how and why they died. We think it is important to remember the lessons learned so we don't repeat them somewhere else, but we'd rather forget the anguish that administered those lessons.

If we have learned anything from our schizophrenia, it's that closure has not come with memorials, or movies, or parades or new military victories. Or with the years that have seen jungles grow back and bomb craters turned into life-giving duck ponds and fish farms.

Then where will we ever find closure? I heard a hint of an answer in the words of Louang Tan when he said, "We must relieve the pain of the victims."

\* \* \* \*

I have come to believe we will never find a healthy, satisfying closure to America's Vietnam War experience until we understand and achieve a very simple, age-old principle. It's a biblical value, taught in both the Old and New Testaments. And surprisingly I've heard many Vietnamese, including several communist officials, call for it when they say, "We need to find reconciliation." But how?

# Part III
## Bridges
## of
## Reconciliation

# 11
## Getting
## Face to Face

I probably should have taken no for an answer. But I was on my second trip back to Vietnam as president of World Vision and in DaNang for the first time since the war. I thought a short side trip to visit the barracks where my Marine squadron had been stationed more than twenty years before would salve my sudden bout of nostalgia.

I told myself it was more than a personal whim; it would provide valuable footage that could be included in the movie we were making about Vietnam, our work there and the ongoing search for a missing peace.

I knew the barracks were still there. I'd seen the buildings when we flew into DaNang. But when I made my request to the local officials, their answer was a quick and emphatic no. The airfield was an off-limits military reservation, they said.

The prudent thing to do would have been to let it drop. A visit to the barracks was hardly essential to the purpose of my visit to Vietnam or to any movie we would put together. But once I had the idea it seemed like a challenge; so I went from official to official asking permission.

Finally, perhaps in frustration, they told me that if I wished, I could make an appointment with the base commander. Only later did I learn Ho Von Quy's reputation as a hard-nosed officer, a man noted for his iron will.

As the car taking me to the airport passed familiar landmarks, my mind went back more than two decades. I recalled the faces of the friends I served with, the feelings of anticipation that came when I strapped myself into the cramped cockpit of an A-6 and prepared for takeoff, the adrenalin-pumping surprise of a midnight mortar attack.

"Thua ong" ("Sir"), called the driver, breaking my reverie. "We here." He pointed to a dingy brick building at the edge of the airfield.

### The Confrontation
Inside, two guards carrying Russian AK-47 rifles ushered me down a bare, echoing hall to the base commander's office. Ho Von Quy sat expressionless behind a long wooden table, impassively studying me as I walked in with my escort from the Ministry of Health. Roughly my age, Commander Ho was short and, for a Vietnamese, stocky. Antagonism flickered in his dark almond eyes. And I felt certain he'd gotten the word that I was some sort of troublemaking American who wanted to ride roughshod over regulations.

Looking at the table between us, I couldn't help thinking of the protracted arguments over the shape of the conference table at the Paris peace talks. But I had no stomach for extended negotiations. So after our formal greetings, I sat down and told him, "I would like permission to visit my old barracks on the far side of the runway."

"No." His eyes flashed. "It cannot be permitted."

In retrospect, and in fairness to the commander, if some Vietnamese visitor to America marched into the commander's office at any U.S. military base and asked to tour one of the buildings accompanied by a video camera crew, any American general would be just as firm. But I wasn't looking at it in those terms that afternoon in DaNang. I explained to the commander the purpose of my visit to his country. I came on a mission of mercy; I was just making this small personal request.

He was implacable. I asked, he said no. I gave another reason and asked again. Back and forth we sparred, but he didn't budge. Shoulders thrust forward in a combative stance, he stared defiantly at me and said with finality, "No!"

I leaned back, staring in return. There was a long silence.

"You were a pilot?" he grunted.

"A bombardier/navigator," I replied. "That's why I want . . ."

"I was a MIG pilot," he interrupted. "I flew out of Hanoi."

"Oh?" I recalled the radio warnings: *Three bandits. Two seven zero. Fifteen miles from bull's-eye.* We always had to know when and where the deadly MIGs were in the air.

"I shot down several of your planes," the commander said matter-of-factly.

"And I dropped more than 1700 tons of bombs on your territory," I countered, wondering whether it was his plane that downed one of my roommates or chased Jim Fickler into Laos.

But as we began to talk about our flying experiences, something happened in that room. We became fellow veterans swapping war stories. I told him about my near miss with a surface-to-air missile, how the pilot flipped us upside-down in a gut-wrenching split-S maneuver and how the rocket, spewing orange flame, flashed past us and disappeared into the night. And I told him about the paralyzing fear I felt before the mission to hit Radio Hanoi.

Ho Van Quy relaxed in his chair, admitting that he too had felt such fear. And the gold in his teeth glinted in an occasional brief smile as our conversation continued. There was no sense of hostility now, as we talked about our war experiences. I had done what I was trained to do and so had he. The war was over.

Gradually the atmosphere in the sparsely furnished room began to change, and an even more meaningful discussion took place. Exactly how the subject came up I don't remember, but we began talking about our children. Commander Ho spoke proudly of his son who had recently become an engineer.

"A fine profession," I said. "My oldest boy is about to graduate from Stanford University. He majored in international relations."

"Good," responded the commander. "Maybe he will help make our world a better place."

By this time we were simply two fathers sharing mutual concerns. The room was quiet again for a moment as we looked out the window, through which the afternoon sun splashed across the room. Then we both spoke at once, blurting out the same hope—that our children would never have to be involved in a war and do what we had to do.

While we talked, the past and its sorrow were forgotten—as was the reason for my visit. We could agree that what mattered now was the future, a time in which our kids could look forward to living together in peace and harmony.

I looked into the face of my former enemy and he looked at me. Again the gold flashed in his smile, and I was reminded of the warmth Christ spoke of when he asked us to love one another— not just our friends but our enemies as well.

Suddenly the compelling desire I had felt to see my old barracks didn't seem so important anymore. I had come searching for reminders of the past but had discovered something far more important: I found a small measure of reconciliation, of healing, of hope for the future.

I stood to bid Commander Ho good-bye and be on my way. But then he did something very uncharacteristic of a Vietnamese. He rose to his feet, walked around the table and threw his arms around me in a huge, impulsive bear hug.

"Come," he said. "I'll take you to the barracks."

\* \* \* \*

I've thought about that experience many times since, as a beautiful illustration of reconciliation between former enemies. And I've thought, *Wouldn't it be wonderful if peoples and countries could come together like that. Maybe then we could bring closure to the Vietnam War.*

Why hasn't it happened?

I've seen some clues in other encounters I've had with government officials from both sides of the Pacific.

### Brick Walls of Bureaucracy

Often after an overseas trip on behalf of World Vision I'll stop in Washington to meet with U.S. officials, to give a report and listen to our government's concerns regarding whatever region of the world I've visited. I don't do this because I feel we need the government's approval for our work, or because American foreign policy will determine what World Vision feels needs to be done. I do it as a matter of diplomacy, to find out whatever helpful information I can and to let our government know about the concerns and work of World Vision. If it helps us avoid stepping on someone's toes or walking into something unaware, I consider it time well spent.

Whenever I've returned from Vietnam, I make it a point to visit the State Department's Southeast Asia desk to update State on World Vision's work in Vietnam, our contacts, our problems and so on. But whenever I've raised the issue of *reconciliation*, and expressed my concerns about the impact our long-term diplomatic and trade embargo has had on the common people of Vietnam, I feel as if I'm talking to a brick wall. Then I invariably get a lecture about Vietnam's failure to abide by the Paris peace accords, the continuing MIA issues, the need for Vietnam to withdraw completely from Cambodia—and now, since Vietnam has pulled out of Cambodia, the necessity of a comprehensive peace in Southeast Asia—along with a list of other examples illustrating Vietnam's recalcitrance. I'm always assured that America's relationship with Vietnam is part of a "complex foreign policy issue."

Invariably I leave the State Department frustrated by my seeming inability to make my concerns heard. But recently, analyzing my reaction after one such visit, I had an insight.

I realized the government and our government officials are focusing on issues, on matters of diplomacy and policy and politics. They aren't seeing the faces of individuals behind the issues—the three-year-old who contracts polio because her country doesn't have an adequate vaccination program for children, the boy who just lost his legs to a land mine buried for a generation, the refugee who is now an American citizen but longs for some word from his loved ones in Vietnam.

A few weeks after reaching this realization I was in Germany for a conference. During a break in our sessions the organizers of the meeting had arranged an afternoon boat trip down the Rhine. We were enjoying the scenery and the beauty of a warm summer day when the boat reached its next stop and who should get aboard but a group of Vietnamese officials. They were in Germany on a visit intended to establish better business and financial ties between the two countries. Heading up the delegation from Hanoi was Vietnam's foreign minister, Nguyen Co Thach.

Thinking what a fortuitous development this was, to have the foreign minister of Vietnam as a captive audience (at least until the boat's next stop), I walked over to introduce myself. I explained that I was president of World Vision, U.S., and had recently visited Vietnam to observe our work there. And I summarized that work.

I expressed my hopes for some kind of reconciliation between our two countries. I told him I had conveyed the same concern to my own government, and I bluntly summarized the reasons the State Department had given me for why that wasn't happening.

Within minutes it was as if we were fighting the war all over again. But what fascinated me was that this Vietnamese communist official was citing the very same issues the State Department had insisted were the barriers to an improved relationship between the countries. He had a different perspective, of course, and different solutions, but he was focusing on the same issues and obviously saw the problem as a complex foreign policy question.

Once again I tried to talk about the needs of the people I'd seen, in America and in Vietnam, who were still being victimized by the war. But I ran into the same brick wall with Foreign Minister Thach that I had at the State Department in Washington. I couldn't seem to penetrate the "issues" with faces.

### Prayers, Politics and Peace
A third encounter, just as telling and at least as troubling, took place a few months later. It occurred at a National Prayer Breakfast where Christian leaders from around the nation had gathered with government leaders in Washington. Table talk focused on: gratitude for a country where we could gather and pray with our leaders; what a wonderful country America is; how great the administration is. And never was heard a discouraging word. Until I spoke up to tell my table host, Deputy Director of the National Security Council Robert Gates (now director of the CIA), that I would like to discuss Vietnam and the need for reconciliation between our two countries.

You'd have thought I was a skunk at a lawn party. The people around our table grew quiet. Mr. Gates launched into the same arguments I'd heard so many times, offering the same East-vs.-West rhetorical baggage that got us into the war in the first place. I tried to talk about the needs and the suffering I'd seen resulting directly and indirectly from our policy. But, in what was meant as the final word on the subject, Mr. Gates looked at me and said with conviction, "Well, we haven't received one letter in that regard."

And that was that.

Why hasn't there been closure? Why haven't the wounds been healed yet? Why are there so many remaining victims from the Vietnam War?

At least part of the answer is that the governments involved, and government officials, both American and Vietnamese, are still focusing on and fighting over issues. For them it remains more a matter of policy and pragmatic politics than of people who suffer.

We long to claim the high moral ground when it comes to American foreign policy. So we point to Vietnam's invasion and occupation of Cambodia, we voice our requirement for a peace that will benefit all of Southeast Asia, we express our moral outrage about the lack of resolution over the MIAs. And we use these legitimate concerns as our excuse for our reluctance to reconcile with Vietnam and as justification for an embargo that has amounted to continuous economic warfare ever since our military efforts failed.

### Sore Losers?

But if we're completely honest with ourselves, we have to admit that one of the considerations here is the fact that Vietnam was the first war America ever lost. It has always been easy for us to play the role of a gracious winner. Being a gracious loser has been far tougher.

We won World War 2 at the cost of more than a million American casualties (dead or wounded), fighting one enemy that prompted our involvement by launching a devastating sneak attack while pretending to negotiate with us and a second enemy that systematically murdered millions of innocent people. But when the war was over we made the Marshall Plan the cornerstone of our nation's foreign policy and helped those ex-enemies rebuild and become two of the most powerful economic powers on earth.

How different has been the aftermath of Vietnam!

Not only was there no Marshall Plan by which we which we tried to help repair and rebuild a country we saw as a battleground, but our embargo policy attempted to prevent other nations from providing any assistance to Vietnam. Instead of helping to heal the wounds, we found it acceptable, even fashionable, to bear a grudge.

Fifteen years after the Allied forces conquered Germany, President Kennedy stood in West Berlin and declared to the world, "I am a Berliner," as an expression of support and friendship with our former enemy in the face of a very real Soviet threat.

Fifteen years after the fall of Saigon we can't even imagine Jane Fonda, let alone a U.S. president, standing in Hanoi and declaring, "I am a Vietnamese!"

In fact, when China, the other communist superpower—angered by its own failed invasion of Vietnam in 1979—threatened the Vietnamese with the vow "We will bleed you white" in Cambodia, the United States backed China! We established a policy of economic and diplomatic boycott designed to do, in a more subtle way perhaps, what China threatened—to drain the very lifeblood out of Vietnam, a nation where half of the population had been our allies. We even went so far as to vote with China to keep the Cambodian seat in the U.N. for the representative of Pol Pot's Khmer Rouge.

As I contrast the aftermaths of World War 2 and Vietnam, it's hard to doubt that revenge is a major factor in our treatment of Vietnam. Oh, I've heard other rationales. But they don't seem nearly as convincing.

One rationale: "The difference is cultural; we have to take into account the difference between the Eastern and Western mindset. You know those Orientals just don't have the same regard for the sanctity of life as we Westerners do."

To this argument I say, "Tell that to the Jews who survived the Holocaust." Sure, we can point to the brutality of Vietnam's re-education camps and the atrocity of Cambodia's killing fields. But as terrible as those things were, they can be no worse than what the Nazis did to the Jews of Europe during World War 2.

And after talking to Vietnamese people, North and South, hearing the pain in their voices and seeing the tears in their eyes as they recall sons and brothers and husbands lost, it's impossible for me to give much credence to this "Oriental disregard for life." Loved ones lost in the war were loved just as much by families and friends on the other side of the Pacific as on this side. And they are just as mourned. Any argument to the contrary is at best ill-informed and at worst rooted in racism.

### Time for Peace?

Another rationale I've heard as for why we haven't tried to establish a relationship with Vietnam is this: "It's a matter of timing. And the time hasn't been right."

This is a harder explanation to swallow with each year that goes by. Nearly two decades have passed since the U.S. pulled its troops out of Vietnam. And still the wounds are not healed.

About fifty per cent of Vietnam's population today was born after the war ended. That means half of all Vietnamese are too young to ever have been our enemies. And of those old enough to even remember the war, half lived in South Vietnam and were our allies. Most of the rest were never active Communists nor fought against any Americans. So only a small fraction of the people now living in Vietnam took any role at all in the war against us.

Yet our punitive economic and diplomatic policy toward Vietnam hurts everyone in the country. And the impact is far greater on those at the bottom of the power structure—the innocent, the young and those who were former allies—than on those few old enemies who remain in power.

So if the relationship of America with Vietnam is a question of timing, it's time to rephrase the question: *What are we waiting for?* How soon will we act to bring healing and closure and end the ongoing suffering of so many millions of victims in Southeast Asia and here at home? How soon will the missing peace be restored?

When I think of healing and the factor of timing, I remember the story of Jesus restoring the withered hand of the man in the synagogue on the Sabbath. The timing couldn't have been worse. Jesus knew the religious leaders were watching and waiting for him to do something they could criticize—like healing a man on the Sabbath, because healing was work and no work was supposed to be done on the Sabbath. But when he saw the man, Jesus didn't tell him to take two aspirin and come back the next morning. He asked the man to stretch out his hand, and when he did, it was restored to normal.

In his compassion, Jesus illustrated the true meaning of restoration—making something new from something old, re-creating the original. He also illustrated something about human suffering and timing. For Jesus, the need for restoration carried a sense of urgency. When he confronted the need, he didn't wait for "better timing." He responded immediately. And in so doing, he provided an example for all of us to follow when we see suffering.

\* \* \* \*

If I learned anything from my experience with my friend Jim Fickler, it's that we never know how much time we have to fulfill our obligation—to do what's right. The day of grace is not forever. The time to act, the time to begin the process of healing, the time to ease the suffering is now.

For the past couple of years a few congressional leaders, including Senator John McCain, himself a former POW in Hanoi, have called for an end to America's economic boycott of Vietnam. General John Vessey, former U.S. Army Chief of Staff, has headed up what has been termed the Vessey initiative, traveling to Vietnam several times in an attempt to establish a cooperative effort between the governments in Washington and Hanoi to resolve any remaining MIA questions as quickly and completely as possible. And recently a number of business interests, including the American Chamber of Commerce, lured by the prospect of economic development in Vietnam and that nation's unexplored oil reserves in the South China Sea, have also begun pressuring the U.S. government to rethink our policy toward Vietnam.

So changes may have begun. But any progress remains slow and very inconsistent. In April 1991, General Vessey returned to Vietnam, the two nations announced the establishment of a U.S. office in Hanoi to work on resolving the remaining MIA cases, and the U.S. rewarded Vietnam's cooperation with the promise of a small (one million dollars) but symbolically significant aid package for Vietnamese people disabled during the war. It was the first financial assistance given to Vietnam by the U.S. government since the war, part of it channeled through World Vision.

And yet, at the very same time as this progress was being made in Vietnam, other U.S. officials were pressuring the Dutch not to lease safer, more modern civilian aircraft to the Vietnamese national airline.

Reconciliation can hardly take place in the face of the mixed messages we communicate through our diplomatic doublespeak.

\* \* \* \*

How and when will the final healing begin? Given our diplomatic history, our focus on policy and politics, and our concern about timing, how can we find closure?

I believe we see the beginning of the answer in the example of Ho Van Quy, the base commander I encountered in DaNang. We started our confrontation on opposite sides of a potentially thorny problem. But in the course of our interaction we began to see each other as individuals. *We looked into each other's faces.* We were then able to talk about our children, our shared hopes and dreams. And then, Commander Ho walked around the table with the divisive issues on it and gave me that big bear hug.

The same holds true in dealing with personal pain. We experience alienation from a family member or friend because of false presuppositions; our relationships at work are disrupted due to lack of understanding of each other's position; arguments and dissension prevail at church as a result of mixed messages and lack of communication. The only way to be reconciled is to get face to face, to look into each other's faces (with the help of a third party if necessary) and to see who the other person is and what we share in common.

Only when we get beyond the problems to see the faces and the needs of others can we get around the issues that separate us and begin to find the kind of personal reconciliation that will lead to the healing we all desire.

# 12
## Getting the
## Feelings
## Out

★

I t's easy for us to forget that a large portion of the Vietnam War was a civil war—Vietnamese against Vietnamese, village neighbor against neighbor, brother against brother. When the war ended for America, our forces came home. But when the war ended in Vietnam, people who had fought and inflicted suffering on each other for years suddenly had to live side by side. Individual Vietnamese were forced to come to grips with the difficult process of reconciliation within their own communities and sometimes within their own families.

I witnessed a powerful example of the successful potential of such reconciliation on a recent visit to the Blind Vocational School of DaNang. After touring this small training facility and marveling at the ability of blind students working in the school's factory to produce rattan furniture and other hand-woven products, I sat in the small administration office and talked with the two men in charge of the school.

The president and the chairman of the school are both blind. Each lost his sight during the war. One, then a member of the Vietcong, lost his sight and part of a hand when he stepped on a land mine. The other, a member of the South Vietnamese Army, had his eyes literally blown out of his face when a shell exploded right in front of him.

These two former enemies are now working side by side every day in an impressive and effective humanitarian effort to help some of the 6,000 blind persons in DaNang province. Their war injuries could have been a permanent barrier, a constant reminder of what once separated them. Instead, their wounds have bound them together; their lives are linked by the reality of their common pain.

That pain has also generated a compassion that transcends the pain. For each of them an attitude of servanthood has emerged over self-interest.

These men who made war are now working together to shape a better peace for others. They offer inspiring proof of the power of reconciliation.

I've thought of those two men many times in the months since I met them. And often I've wondered, *If that kind of healing, that quality of reconciliation, can take place between two individuals, why can't it happen on a broader scale—between America and Vietnam?*

The conclusion I've come to is that the obstacles to reconciliation between peoples and between nations are usually the same barriers that prevent reconciliation and healing between individuals— between husbands and wives, parents and children, between neighbors and between coworkers. So let's consider those hurdles.

The first is the deep emotional scarring. I was reminded again recently of the intense emotional fallout that remains for so many people.

* * * *

We had offered meeting space at our World Vision headquarters in Southern California for a group called "Point Man Ministries" to hold a regional convention. Point Man Ministries is a Christian organization founded by and for Vietnam vets, to establish a network of small support groups—groups designed to help one another cope with the emotional and physical wounds resulting from the war.

My only responsibility at this conference was to attend the opening session and, on behalf of World Vision, to welcome the conferees to our building. An opening prayer was followed by a song by a soloist who, judging from her introduction, was well known to the group.

She sang about "broken faces."

And by the time she finished, a majority of those seated around that room, many of whom were in wheelchairs, were openly weeping. Convincing proof that even today, twenty to twenty-five years and more after the war ended for these veterans, the deepest emotions they've ever known in their lives still lie just beneath the surface, ready to erupt.

In our discussion of the various victims of the war in Section II of this book, we mentioned feelings such as grief, disappointment, bitterness and despair. I suspect all those feelings played a part in the reaction of the vets attending that conference.

There are other emotional reactions that also serve as common obstacles in the road to reconciliation in the aftermath of any conflict. And one of the most common is anger.

### A Lot to Be Angry About
Psychologists tell us anger can be a very natural and understandable response to the experience of frustration, pain and/or fear. Conflict, whether interpersonal or international, can create all three.

The Vietnam War certainly produced a surplus of frustration: for an American military that felt it wasn't allowed to do what was needed in order to win; for those who fought and saw friends die for a cause ultimately deemed "not worth finishing"; for the disillusioned on all sides; and for all those victims in Vietnam and America who still see little hope for closure and no end in sight for their suffering.

All the victims we talked about in chapters 5-10 illustrate the pain of war.

And then there's fear, which didn't stop when the war ended. The fear of facing and dealing with the residual pain. And even the fear that if you make the first step toward reconciliation you could be hurt again.

The administrators of the vocational school for the blind certainly must have known fear—the fear of an uncertain future and not knowing how well they could cope with it. The one who fought with the South Vietnamese army had to be afraid that he might not even get a chance to rebuild his life. After all, those are the rules of the game: To the victors belong the spoils; the losers go to re-education camps.

Those two blind ex-enemies would have known all three reasons for anger: fear, pain and tremendous frustration. Yet they overcame it all.

### Too Tired to Care
Apathy is another common barrier to reconciliation. At first glance it seems just the opposite of deep emotions. Yet it sometimes follows close on the heels of feelings of anger. It may be a defense mechanism, a denial of the strong emotion. Or it could be a backlash, a pendulum swing the other way once anger and other intense feelings begin to fade or come under control.

Strong emotions can take their toll on us in the wake of conflict.

They wear us down to the point that we quit wrestling with them, give an exhausted sigh and say, "I'm tired of the hassle. I just don't care anymore."

The blind men I met in DaNang didn't have the luxury of apathy. It's more of an option for those who can withdraw and put a measure of distance between themselves and the conflict. So apathy has more potential as a barrier to reconciliation for Americans.

In fact, it may be a very real danger in the wake of the Gulf War, which so many hope has once and for all "exorcised the ghost of Vietnam." An apathetic isolation could easily replace the deliberate diplomatic isolation we've inflicted on Vietnam since the war ended—with the same painful effect on the common people of the country. If that happens, it will hinder reconciliation and the hope for closure will be further delayed.

### A Child Shall Lead Them

One more obstacle to reconciliation was illustrated for me in an experience that took place on my very first trip back to Vietnam in 1988. World Vision had been invited by the country's Ministry of Health to provide help in the area of rehabilitation and prosthetics. While we were intrigued and excited about the opportunity, we remained wary of the communist government and its motives. We didn't yet know how well we could work with the bureaucracy in Hanoi or how accountable they would be to us for the materials we provided.

We didn't have much in the way of precedent to go on. Hanoi was only beginning to open up to the West. The Vessey initiative had only just begun. And we were among the first NGOs (non-government organizations) granted permission to begin work in the country.

We carried with us on that first trip a letter of introduction from Ronald Reagan. In retrospect, it may not have been the wisest strategy to rely on a recommendation from the most outspoken adversary of Communism at that time to get us off on the right foot with the Marxist bureaucracy in Hanoi! But we wanted to be taken seriously. And given Vietnam's police-state paranoia and history of duplicity at the negotiating table, I felt a little more secure with a letter reminding anyone we might unintentionally offend that we had the clout of the American presidency behind us. And our government knew we were there.

However, I'm not sure Reagan's letter helped at all. It may well have made it harder for the Ministry of Health officials to distinguish between the American government which continued to blackball Vietnam in the international community and our American-based organization that wanted only to render humanitarian aid. The defenses were definitely up in our first meeting in Hanoi. I was accompanied that day by World Vision's Southeast Asia director who was coordinating our new work in Vietnam from his office in Bangkok. Also at the meeting were the editor of our World Vision publications, my wife, Margaret Ann, and my son, Jesse.

The atmosphere in the room was extremely confrontational. This despite our best efforts to clearly position ourselves as an NGO, with no ties to the U.S. government or American foreign policy. It seemed the mere fact of our nationality inspired these communist officials to rhetorically unload on us a message they obviously wanted us to deliver for them in Washington. They wanted to make it abundantly clear who was in charge and what their requirements would be.

Official notetakers recorded every word. Tensions ran high. It was not a positive meeting.

As the minister in charge of the meeting brought it to a close he asked, "Does anyone here have anything else to say?"

Silence met the question. There seemed nothing to add to such an unsatisfying encounter.

Then I heard the uncertain voice of my twelve-year-old son. "Yeah, I do."

All the eyes in the room turned toward the end of the table where Jesse sat. *What in the world is Jesse going to say?* I couldn't imagine.

He seemed for a moment as if he wished he could take back his words. But then he looked around the room at those communist officials and began: "I just want to say that I know my dad. He came here only because World Vision wants to help the people of Vietnam. And he wants to help. I think you should let him. You can trust him."

That was it. The meeting ended with our Vietnamese counterparts beaming from ear to ear and clustering around Jesse to shake his hand and have their photographs taken with him. The ice was broken, the atmosphere changed, and that was the turning point in our relationship with the government in a visit that was to provide the foothold for expanding World Vision's work in Vietnam.

The lesson for me was as striking as the irony. Here we had two groups of officials, each with their own interests and agendas. One side spoke with the authority of the nation of Vietnam; the other carried a letter from the most powerful individual in the world. And we found ourselves at an absolute impasse.

Until a twelve-year-old kid with no authority, no portfolio, the only one in the room obviously devoid of self-interest, became an agent of reconciliation with an honest expression of his feelings and his concern.

**Pride Prolongs the Pain**
I saw in that incident the very antithesis of yet another common barrier to reconciliation.

Pride. The deadliest of human sins. Self-centered, self-interested, self-concerned pride. The root of human stubbornness. Holding to entrenched positions to protect individual and corporate egos.

If we're honest, we have to admit pride is a major bugaboo, perhaps the most common of all barriers to reconciliation. It keeps us from apologizing to our spouses, forgiving those who wrong us, making the first move to repair and rebuild a damaged relationship.

Certainly pride has prolonged the pain of the Vietnam War. Two decades ago, pride prolonged the Paris peace talks. While pride made the shape of a conference table the metaphor for competing ideologies, thousands of people continued to die.

Today, we have a new "table." We now argue over the sequence of steps necessary for a comprehensive peace in Southeast Asia. The Vietnamese insist that a normalization of relationships with America and an end to the economic boycott will enhance the peace prospects. The United States wants it the other way around: first peace, a comprehensive peace in Cambodia; then a normalized relationship.

Impasse. Pride in the guise of *realpolitik* impacts the lives of innocent people, prolonging the grudge America bears and further fueling the stubbornness of the Vietnamese. Reconciliation is delayed. And the pain continues on both sides of the Pacific.

## Overcoming the Barriers

How do we get past pride and all the other barriers to reconciliation?

I see the answer to that question in the examples of my son Jesse and the two blind colleagues at that DaNang Vocational School.

We may be talking about armies and nations; we may be talking about families and individuals. Becoming reconciled after some sort of hostility has divided us requires a drastic change in our focus. We must *look beyond our own concerns and selfish interests.* Beyond our own feelings, our own agenda, our own position, policies and politics.

Like the blind educators we must look beyond our own suffering to *find and acknowledge a shared pain.*

And then we must *respond to someone else's need.*

In the aftermath of any painful conflict, especially when the deepest wounds remain raw and exposed, the smallest step toward reconciliation can seem both naive and risky. As naive as a twelve-year-old kid standing up at the end of a frustrating session of negotiations to ask a group of suspicious and belligerent communist bureaucrats to trust his dad's motives. As risky as one blind man sharing a dream and trusting his life to another blind man who used to be his sworn and bitter enemy.

But in such naiveté, such risk, may lie our best and perhaps our only hope for ever finding healing for the conflicts that separate family members, friends and nations.

# 13

# A New
# Openness

nother major barrier to reconciliation and healing from the
wounds of conflict is a sense of helplessness. The other
party has not shown good faith, perhaps deceiving,
double-crossing or lying about us. So we let the circumstances
discourage us. We think, *The conflict has lasted so long. The hurts go
too deep! The problems are too big, the differences between us too great.
At this time, there's just no solution.*

When I hear this sort of sentiment, when I feel this way myself,
I'm reminded of a poignant image I've pictured in my mind so often
since a friend of mine told me this story, shared with him by a nurse
who worked in a California hospital.

One ward of this hospital housed a number of severely handicapped Vietnam vets, a number of whom were multiple amputees.
Some of these injured vets had suffered so much pain, frustration,

anger and despair over the years that they had withdrawn into a protective shell of silence, refusing to acknowledge or respond to those around them.

On another ward in this same hospital were several terminally ill infants. The staff could feed and change them and provide for their ongoing medical care. But, as is the case in so many hospitals, there just wasn't the personnel needed to provide these children with all the individual attention and the one-on-one human contact they needed in the final months, weeks and days of their lives.

Then a nurse came up with a very unorthodox proposal. It was discussed and instituted on a trial basis. For several hours a day, terminally ill babies in desperate need of human contact were brought to the veterans' ward to be held by these emotionally withdrawn amputees. Babies rested in the laps of wheelchair-bound patients. They were placed in the hospital beds beside men who couldn't get up into wheelchairs. And in at least one case a baby was actually strapped across the torso of a man with no arms.

That's the image that sticks in my mind. An armless vet providing skin-to-skin contact for a terminally ill child. The seemingly helpless giving comfort to the hopeless. And vice versa. For as those vets gave of themselves to the children, the babies ministered to the men. Within three days the vets were talking again. In reaching out to others, these men, who had every reason to believe they had nothing to give, discovered a renewed sense of self-worth.

Many times since I've heard that story I've seen situations where there is massive emotional, physical or financial need, and my first reaction has been to think, *Nothing can be done. The resources just aren't there.* But I keep being convicted and challenged by the thought of what took place in that hospital.

If an armless vet can reach out and comfort a dying baby, how can I see the hurt and the pain caused by unreconciled conflict and say, "I can't do a thing. I don't have enough resources."

It's an easy and common excuse. But it's usually just an excuse. The first steps toward reconciliation and healing seldom require much in the way of resources.

What does it take?

We talked in the last chapter about the need for courage and for a change of focus from self to others. For the handicapped vets, as with the two blind Vietnamese educators, this was made easier with the recognition of a shared pain.

We spent six chapters, the entire second section of this book, establishing the basis of shared pain as a result of the Vietnam War. The need for healing and reconciliation in this scenario should be obvious.

## One Last Chance

So what else will it take to find the missing peace? Three factors.

The first requirement for reconciliation is *opportunity*.

We've missed a lot of opportunities for reconciliation in Vietnam over the past twenty years. But the opportunities we face in the nineties may be even better than the ones we missed in the seventies and eighties.

Vietnam today seems poised on the verge of a potential economic revolution. When I first returned in 1988 the nation's economy seemed paralyzed by a crippling combination of runaway inflation (up to one thousand per cent a year) and a national infrastructure devastated by decades of war and neglect. An aura of economic hopelessness pervaded the country, especially the North.

That is changing. Gradually the infrastructure is being repaired and rebuilt. And despite America's continued discouragement of our allies' investments in Vietnam, the Japanese and Europeans are now all over the country; I've noticed more of them with each of my visits. They're obviously anxious and willing to exploit Vietnam's large and trainable low-cost work force.

As of spring 1991, over two hundred international companies, seventy from Japan, have made investments in Vietnam. So far most of the investments are small, but these nations obviously want to have a foot in the door in order to get a leg up on U.S. interests whenever we call off the embargo and the Vietnamese economy takes off.

However, the biggest and most surprising economic changes I've seen in Vietnam are taking place at the grassroots. For despite the Communists' firm grip on the government in Hanoi and a totalitarian bureaucracy as committed as ever to the principles of Marxism, capitalism is fast becoming the choice of the people.

The South, which experienced a Western-based economy for years, has always had a strong and active black market and provided fertile ground for local entrepreneurs. But what has amazed me on my most recent trips to Vietnam has been the change in the North. Even in Hanoi it seems every other family now owns its own shop, producing goods and income, creating capital. All the businesses I saw were labor-intensive; the people have a mind to work. Looking around, you get the idea that given half a chance, the country's economy will really flourish. The government, desperate for financial resources, may give it that chance; it often looks the other way and in some cases unofficially encourages such initiative.

Even if the government wanted to stop it, too many people are now involved in capitalistic ventures for the communist rulers to control their efforts. Governmental middle managers are themselves becoming entrepreneurs. They're finding ways to extend health care, improve education and harvest better crops. More of the common people are finding ways of "making it"; in the process, the state's bureaucracy is becoming more and more irrelevant and impotent.

However, the grassroots economic surge has yet to trickle up to the government. The nation as a whole is financially and economically strapped. Vietnam still can't afford to provide its own people with basic social services. Sixteen years after taking over Saigon, this is a government that still cannot serve its citizens. For this Vietnam is almost totally dependent on outside help.

In many cases the central government has told its various ministry departments to establish their own contacts and develop their own relationships with outside organizations such as World Vision. As a result, agencies like UNICEF and World Vision are doing more for the Vietnamese people than the government can do.

So both the government and the private sector in Vietnam present new and unprecedented opportunities for the kind of interaction, encouragement and support that can promote new relationships, healing and reconciliation.

### The Year of the Tourist

A related development that impacts the new opportunities in Vietnam is the country's renewed interest in promoting tourism. There was a gradual but definite loosening of travel restrictions at the end of the eighties. Vietnam even declared 1990 as "The Year of the Tourist." In the wake of Tienanmen Square and the anti-communist movements that toppled governments in Eastern Europe, Hanoi became a bit paranoid and clamped back down for a time. But then things seemed to ease again.

The welcome the Vietnamese now extend to Westerners, particularly Americans, was exemplified in an encounter I had on my most recent trip. We were in Bangkok, about to board an old Vietnamese airliner for Hanoi when a man about my age came up to me in the airport. He was Vietnamese and approached us politely, wishing only to converse with a few Americans.

He explained that he worked for the Vietnamese government and was responsible for handling the visa requests of foreign travelers. He quickly, proudly pointed out how the process was becoming less cumbersome and more encouraging of outside guests.

Inevitably we got around to asking the question, "Were you involved in the war?" Softly, matter-of-factly, this man (whose name I will protect) told us his story. He said he crossed over the border into South Vietnam in 1964. He fought in the South for more than four years and then was critically wounded during the famous Tet offensive. A U.S. Marine, in an engagement just west of DaNang, caught him in the sights of an M-79 grenade launcher. He almost died on the spot, his entire right side shredded by steel fragments.

He nearly died several times on the long road back to Hanoi. The Ho Chi Minh Trail was the only artery north, and it was neither safe nor short. I know, because I bombed it on several occasions during that very time period. He spent three long months on the trail before he reached the North and recovered in the relative safety of Hanoi.

But his badly broken body came home to a broken country. The sacrifice of four years yielded little. He lost his health, his youth, his innocence and his ideals. Even the peace that came when Saigon fell was soon lost as his nation found itself in a new two-front war with Cambodia and China.

Yet as I talked with this former enemy, I sensed no bitterness, no anger.

A nation needs to be rebuilt. A world needs reconciliation. And so this Vietnamese man helps people, even those who once tried to kill him, to come to his country and see his people.

It's that kind of welcome, from individual Vietnamese as well as a government hungry for foreign currency, that provides a wide open door of opportunity in Vietnam today—an opportunity for reconciliation and healing.

Yet another development that has enhanced the opportunity for reconciliation with Vietnam is the cataclysmic collapse of Communism in Eastern Europe and the present turmoil within the republics of the former Soviet Union. The forced ending of Vietnam's long dependence on trade and military backing from the Soviet bloc may well create a vacuum to be filled by anyone willing to show a commitment and interest in Vietnam.

## Help for the Churches

Another opportunity we're excited about at World Vision is the opportunity to begin working with and through the church in Vietnam. Persecution continues. But in some areas and among some government officials there's a begrudging respect for the church—its resiliency and integrity.

In developing plans for improving medical services in one province of the country, we actually had a government leader suggest we talk to some local church officials to get a broader perspective on the needs and problems of the people. We are still wary of drawing too much attention to or casting suspicion on the church in Vietnam, so we are proceeding slowly and judiciously. But we have begun to work through some Vietnamese churches to provide economic assistance in the form of sewing machines to establish small tailoring businesses, and we're hoping soon to provide a number of old, foot-pump organs to some churches to enhance their worship experiences.

It seems everywhere you look in Vietnam you can see new openings, new possibilities for reaching out in big and little acts of reconciliation. The opportunity is definitely there.

## Needed: Good Examples

So, in addition to opportunity, what else is needed ?

The second requirement for reconciliation to take place is good *models*. Examples to show the way.

We're getting more of those in Vietnam all the time. World Vision certainly is not the only group engaged in acts of reconciliation in Vietnam.

Our sister organization, World Relief, an agency of the National Association of Evangelicals, works directly with the Vietnamese, primarily in the area of refugee orientation and resettlement. The Christian and Missionary Alliance denomination, which had extensive work in Vietnam before and during the war, is working on finding new and better ways for Western Christians to relate to and help the church in Vietnam. And another Christian organization, Vets with a Mission, has sent short-term work teams into Vietnam to help with a variety of humanitarian efforts, including construction and repair work at a children's polio center.

On one of my trips, I ran into some former members of a U.S. Army Corps of Engineers battalion who had returned to Vietnam, as civilians and volunteers, with a set of old maps for the dangerous task of locating and disarming mine fields they had laid near the DMZ twenty years before.

Numerous NGOs (non-government organizations) have established their own programs in and for Vietnam. Operation Smile sends teams of volunteer medical personnel to work with Vietnamese plastic surgeons to correct cleft palates and lip conditions among Vietnamese children. Groups such as Need International, Project Concern International, and the U.S. Committee for Scientific Cooperation with Vietnam each sponsor their own medical-assistance and child-survival programs. And there are many more organizations, all of which provide examples and contribute to the cause of reconciliation between the people of America and the people of Vietnam.

At World Vision we're especially excited about the re-establishment of a child-sponsorship program in Vietnam. Prior to 1975, we sponsored up to 40,000 children there, many of them in orphanages around Saigon. All of that came to an end when the South fell to the Communists. But we have recently begun a new child sponsorship program through the Thuy An Center, a facility that houses and cares for handicapped children.

We have also provided individual Americans with another opportunity for personal acts of reconciliation through our one-on-one mentoring program for Amerasian refugees. The Amerasians and other Vietnamese refugees among us serve as natural bridges of reconciliation between our two countries. Opportunities to establish friendships and respond to their needs are numerous.

So, there are many practical models of reconciliation that can both inspire us and point the way to more and bigger steps.

### Need a Reason?

We see the need. We have the opportunity to act and the models to follow. Reconciliation is within our ability to do. So what else do we need?

The third requirement is *motive*. We've got to have a reason, got to be convinced it's worth all the effort and risk. We have to have an answer to the question: *Why should we be reconciled with our enemies, those who have hurt us, those we have hurt?*

The first answer to that is: "Because it's good for us."

Just as it is physically easier to smile than it is to frown and emotionally healthier to love than to hate, so it is better for us to be reconciled than unreconciled.

This is true on an individual level, between spouses and in-laws and coworkers and neighbors. But it's just as true when we are talking about conflicts between nations and peoples. President Chamorro of Nicaragua evidently understood it when she said in her inaugural address: "Reconciliation is much more beautiful than winning."

Living in peace rather than hostility is good for us. And in the process of working toward reconciliation, we will learn much about ourselves. We'll come face to face with our limits, our strengths and our weaknesses. We'll discover whether or not we can overcome our emotions. We can do it out of a motive of self-interest if for no other reason.

* * * *

But for those of us who call ourselves Christians, or take seriously the claim that America is a Christian nation, there is a second and even more compelling motive for pursuing the goal of reconciliation. It has to do with being like the One whom we follow.

For me it is all summed up in two crucial questions posed to me by two friends from opposite sides of the world.

# 14
# What Would
# Jesus Do?

The chief reason Christians work toward reconciliation—personal, racial, national, international—is that Jesus did so. If we are to be his followers, we too must be peacemakers.
Two questions have made me think hard about my responsibility here.

The first crucial question is borrowed from a good friend, the always outspoken Christian social activist, speaker and author, Tony Campolo. But to understand the full impact this question has for me, I must relate the painfully memorable circumstances under which Tony first posed it for me.

During my tenure as president of Eastern College and Seminary in Pennsylvania, Tony was a prominent member of our faculty. And on this particular occasion we were invited to share the speaking platform one evening in nearby Lancaster.

I was slated to speak first. The young man who introduced me seemed enamored by my military experience. He briefly cited my current role at Eastern and then gave the audience a detailed accounting of my former role as a U.S. Marine captain during the Vietnam War—a bombardier/navigator who flew three hundred combat missions in an A-6 aircraft, recipient of 28 Air Medals, the Distinguished Flying Cross and so on. He did everything but strike up a band to play the Marine Corps hymn.

Such an introduction would have been a little embarrassing even under the best of circumstances, say at an American Legion rally. But in Lancaster, the heart of pacifist Mennonite country, it was disastrous. The longer my introducer went on, the more little Mennonite caps I spotted in the crowd and the more I sensed the audience slipping away from me. By the time I stepped up to the podium I felt as welcome as a warmonger at a convention for pacifists. I managed to speak briefly, to a less-than-enthusiastic audience, before returning to my platform seat.

Then it was Tony's turn. And he decided to relate the full account of his own military experience.

On the verge of being drafted during the Korean War, Tony had been required to visit a local recruitment office to fill out some paperwork. When he finished the forms and turned them in to the officer in charge, he said: "I feel I need to tell you something."

"What's that?" the man wanted to know.

"Well," said Tony. "I think I could go through boot camp with little problem. And I could learn to shoot a rifle in target practice. But you need to understand that if I was ever in combat and the time came for me to point my rifle at another human being and pull the trigger, I don't think I could do that."

"And why not?" the officer wanted to know.

"You see," Tony answered, "I'm a Christian."

"Well," the military man responded testily, "what's that got to do with shooting someone?"

Tony replied, "What that means is that for me there will come a time when I have to stop and ask the question, 'What would Jesus do?' "

Now the officer was indignant. "That's ridiculous. Everyone knows what Jesus would do!"

At that point in the story, Tony paused to let his point sink in. We all should know what Jesus would do. It was obvious!

"Would Jesus point his rifle at an enemy and pull the trigger? Would Jesus drop bombs on his enemies?" As Tony asked this last question he turned and looked toward me. I wanted to sink through the floor. But I have to give Tony credit: he had that Mennonite crowd well in hand and received rousing applause when he finished speaking.

Tony and his wife, Peggy, had accompanied Margaret Ann and me to Lancaster that evening. The return drive to Philadelphia seemed exceedingly long and quiet. "Aren't the stars beautiful tonight?" was about the extent of the conversation as I remember it.

I assume Peggy, the always-sensitive member of the Campolo family, must have talked to Tony after they got home that night. Because the next morning, when I walked into my office in Eastern's administration building, there was a letter waiting for me on my desk. It was a handwritten apology from Tony, asking my forgiveness for his insensitivity the night before.

I promptly forgave him (though forgetting has been a little tougher!). And sometime later, when I heard Tony lamenting that he seemed to spend half his life apologizing, I confess my first reaction was to think to myself, *You probably ought to!*

But the question Tony posed that night has been even more memorable than the speaking experience I've tried for so long to forget. "What would Jesus do?"

That is a question we all should ask in every situation, with every decision we face in life. But it has special significance for the subject of reconciliation.

**Not Optional**

The first work of the Christian gospel, the central point of the cross, is reconciliation. It's why Christ came to earth to live and die in our place. But it was never meant to stop there. As the apostle Paul wrote in 2 Corinthians 5:18, "All this is from God, who reconciled us to himself through Christ and gave us the ministry of reconciliation."

There is a lot of Scripture evidence that those who claim to follow Christ are expected to be reconcilers as well. In other words, if our relationship to God is right, it will make a difference in our relationships with others.

According to 1 John 4:20, "If anyone says, 'I love God,' yet hates his brother, he is a liar. For anyone who does not love his brother, whom he has seen, cannot love God, whom he has not seen."

God does not even find our worship acceptable unless we are reconciled to others. In Matthew 5:23-24 Jesus said, "If you are offering your gift at the altar and there remember that your brother has something against you, leave your gift there in front of the altar. First go and be reconciled to your brother; then come and offer your gift."

John Perkins, who suffered persecution and vicious beating during the sixties as a black man and civil rights advocate in rural Mississippi, cites all these Scriptures and more in his book *Justice for All.* Then he concludes, "To be reconciled to my brother I must first be reconciled with God; to remain reconciled to God, I must be reconciled to my brother. I cannot have one without the other."

Christians wondering what they should do when confronted with the wounds and pain of conflict—whether national or personal—have only to consider the question, "What would Jesus do?"

If we submit to the lordship of a reconciling Savior who gave his life in the ultimate act of reconciliation, what choice do we have when we're faced with a need and an opportunity for reconciliation? If God thought the principle of reconciliation important enough to die for, it should be our duty and desire to help bring reconciliation wherever there has been hurt and conflict.

What would Jesus do?

I still wrestle with that question as it relates to my own involvement in the Vietnam War. But just as Christians have debated for ages the "Christian view of war," just as pundits still argue the right and wrong of American involvement in Vietnam, we could debate forever what kind of reconciliation might have been possible back in the sixties.

But the picture is clearer today. There's little room for argument if we honestly try to answer the question, "What would Jesus do in Vietnam today?"

If Jesus came today to see all the vets still traumatized by the war, the families separated, the children left behind, all those who continue to grieve over the MIAs, and the millions of innocent people who still suffer the tragic repercussions of the Vietnam War, what would he do? He would call for reconciliation and do whatever he could to bring it about. As he did when he healed the man with the withered hand on the Sabbath, he wouldn't wait: he would seize the first opportunity to begin the restoration process and make all these lives whole again.

If we believe that, we can do no less.

### A Convicting Question

What would Jesus do? In trying to answer that question I'm forced to consider a second one. This one was posed to me by another friend—in Vietnam. I know this man is my friend because he told me so. I ran into him on the streets of Ho Chi Minh City. I was in search of quiet time for reflection alone in a city park. He was looking to talk to an American.

We spent an hour together, and he told me his story. He had served in the South Vietnamese army as one of our allies. We taught him English, we subsidized his pay, showed him how to shoot and secured his trust. In 1972 we turned the war over to his people.

When the South Vietnamese government collapsed in 1975 and some of the generals, dignitaries and high officials were flown out of Saigon to start a new life in the U.S. or other countries, this man was one of the hundreds of thousands of allies left behind.

He was sent to a re-education camp. The forced labor imposed on him for his Western ties extended to his wife, a frail woman who ultimately contracted malaria during the long hours of toil in the rice paddies.

Following his release from the camp, the husband was told he could never again hold a meaningful job in Vietnam. Today his wife remains too sick to work and he labors as a cyclo driver, earning only pennies a day for biking passengers around the city. He has four children. The family is financially destitute. My friend clearly felt grateful for the opportunity to talk to an American. Before he left me there in the park, he promised to come by my hotel the next day with his cyclo to take me all around the city and show me the new sights. He said he wouldn't charge me anything. I thanked him but said that of course I would want to pay him.

He protested, with words that cut right to my heart:

*"Let me do this for you. After all, what are friends for?"*

We had made his country a battleground. We had promised to protect his interests, made him dependent on us, convinced him to choose our side, asked him to trust us. Then we changed our minds and deserted him, letting him suffer the pain of defeat. And we have pretty much ignored his suffering (when we weren't adding to it with diplomatic and economic embargoes) ever since.

And yet, after all that, my friend offers to make a genuine sacrifice to do me a kindness and asks me, "What are friends for?"

**A Parallel Parable**

His convicting question made me think of another man, a certain man on his way from Jerusalem to Jericho. On his way, robbers fell upon him, beat him and left him financially destitute. His health was destroyed in the violence. His very life was made tenuous by events larger than he could control. He was abandoned along the road, isolated in his pain and agony.

It was Jesus who told this familiar story, in response to a question very similar to my Vietnamese friend's question, "What are friends for?" Jesus was answering the question, "Who is my neighbor?"

Jesus' story of the Good Samaritan tells us that neighborliness and friendship require more than piety and religious pronouncements. They demand overt acts of compassion—acts of healing and reconciliation.

In our fractured personal and family relationships, in situations of racial misunderstanding and hostility, on both the worldwide level and the very personal one, these acts of compassion are absolutely necessary. And they will cost you something. They will involve time, sometimes time you don't think you can spare. They will be inconvenient, sometimes embarrassing. There is risk; what if your efforts are misunderstood or rejected? Even if something is accomplished, you may never get thanked.

I'd like to update Jesus' parable and identify some of the parallel characters in the Vietnam drama. The passing of time and the perspective of history make it a little easier. We can better tell today, for example, who the robbers are.

For starters, there is the bankrupt Marxist ideology that stole the hopes of the populace years ago but unfortunately remains very much in control. Then, there is the paralyzed bureaucracy of a centralized government that has attempted to squeeze out the last ounce of individual incentive.

Another robber is the illusion of a defensive war, an ironic exercise that led Vietnam to ever-increasing offensive warfare. Vietnam today still maintains one of the largest standing armies in the world, a totalitarian "necessity" that robs the people of vital human services. There is also a cold-blooded mindset that has allowed the dead bodies of MIAs to become bargaining chips in governmental affairs. Finally there remains the Vietnamese stubbornness that engages in lengthy negotiations even while some of its own people are starving to death—the very same stubbornness that won the war but has lost the peace.

All these forces have robbed and continue to rob the Vietnamese people. But we need to be even-handed.

There are also robbers on this side of the Pacific. One of them is the simplistic foreign policy of our own global superpower. We see so much in East-West terms, failing to notice the intense nationalism of the smaller nations. When we assigned our simplistic foreign policy to the Vietnamese, we stole some of their independent identity. We created South Vietnam's dependency on massive aid, and once we had them hooked on it, we up and walked away. We broke our commitment when social and political pressures here at home prompted us to make a face-saving exit from that part of the world.

We also had a mentality that treated the rest of Southeast Asia as a mere "side show" to the main event—the war in Vietnam. That's why some of the responsibility for what happened in Cambodia is ours. Because we devalued Asian life, we justified turning our backs on an entire region of the world, permitting our allies to languish in re-education camps and allowing a holocaust to take place next door in Cambodia. Ultimately we robbed Vietnam of the opportunity for normalization with the West, when we played the China card against the Soviets in the late seventies. We judged the continuation of the cold war to be more important than bringing the Vietnam War to closure.

So the thieves and the robbers come from both sides of the Pacific. As do the victims. We've already spent a major portion of the book identifying the victims, so let's move on to the other characters in the drama. Who are the passers-by? Who will play the role of the Good Samaritan?

We have to admit that America has filled the first role. For nearly twenty years we have passed by the Vietnam issue on the far side of the road. Or, more literally, on this side of the ocean. We've left a wounded, bleeding country lying in Southeast Asia and gone busily, blissfully on our way toward the twenty-first century.

And what about the religious establishment, the church in the West? Why has the Western church been silent and unresponsive? Is it simply because we haven't known? Is Vietnam too far back on the road of our memories? Are the memories too painful? Is love impossible, forgiveness too difficult to bestow on our former enemies? Could our patriotism and our national pride be stronger than our Christian commitment? Is the kingdom of earth more important than the kingdom of God? Is the church so insulated from the world that we can't see the hurting victims in our midst?

For whatever reason, we have for the most part passed by on the other side. We have remained silent.

*   *   *   *

"What are friends for?"

We hear the clear answer to that in Jesus' Good Samaritan parable. We are called to reach out in compassion to anyone who hurts, even our enemies.

"What would Jesus do?"

That's a tough question because the answer is so easy. We see it in Jesus' example, in his life and in his death. It was Jesus who, when he looked down from the cross at the people who had driven

181

the nails through his hands and his feet, called out to God, "Lord, erase it from your mind. Lord, forget it. Make believe it never happened, Lord. Forgive them. They don't know what they are doing."

In his death on the cross, Jesus put into practice everything he preached, everything he was and everything he came to be. It was and is history's most impressive example of reconciliation.

## A Vietnamese Parable

But next to that, perhaps the most beautiful example of reconciliation I've ever heard about took place in Vietnam. I learned the story and witnessed its results on one of my most recent visits.

It was Easter week. The time in the annual Christian calendar when we remember the greatest love story ever told, that most perfect example of reconciliation.

I was in DaNang. Sitting at a small wooden table in a most humble dwelling, listening to a father tenderly tell the story of the fifteen-year-old boy sitting beside him.

It was truly beautiful to watch this father talk to this boy and about him. His eyes said it all; they spoke of so much compassion and love.

The child needed all of both. For he was blind and mentally retarded.

The relationship between the man and the boy was a miracle in itself. It seems that in the last turbulent days of the war, this man's wife had a brief affair with another man. She became pregnant. By the time the infant was born, a healthy, perfect little baby boy, her remorse was so great she wanted to kill the child.

She almost succeeded. She slipped out of the house, walked to a remote spot in the bush, dug a shallow grave, and buried the child alive. But her husband was already looking for her, and he finally found her bending over a fresh mound of dirt. Working feverishly, he dug the baby out of the ground. But not before the lack of oxygen had rendered the child permanently blind and severely retarded.

The man took his distraught wife and the broken child home. He gave the boy a name, his name—Tran Dinh Loi. He loved the boy as his own son, and his love for his wife transcended the enormity of her sin.

In the intervening years, a gift developed in the young lad, the gift of a beautiful voice. He used it to sing Vietnamese love songs to us as we sat at the table in his home. He sang softly with a wide-open smile completely filling his face, his head bobbing from side to side with the music—a Vietnamese Stevie Wonder. And when he was singing, with his father's hand gently resting on his arm to give him little pats and squeezes of encouragement and reassurance, we couldn't help but feel the love and compassion of the adopted father flowing through this young life.

A scandalous birth emerged out of the brokenness of a fallen world. Sin was buried in a grave that ultimately could not contain the body. That body was rescued by a father whose love was greater than his personal pain. An unfaithful wife was completely forgiven; her sins were remembered no more.

We sat around a small wooden table and listened to a child's love songs. A true Easter song of incomprehensible love, forgiveness and reconciliation.

This example of an earthly father's love and forgiveness, like the example of a heavenly Father's love as illustrated in the original Easter story, inspires and challenges me. If reconciliation can take place in circumstances like those experienced by this Vietnamese father, it can take place in any personal relationship marked by conflict and hurt.

In thinking about this father's love as shown in his eyes and his compassionate touch, I'm reminded of another touch which I myself experienced in Vietnam, the bear hug bestowed on me by Ho Van

Quy, the commander of the DaNang airfield.

These two beautiful examples of reconciliation give me hope. They remind me that God is in the business of promoting giant and spontaneous bear hugs.

He calls all of us who want to follow him to a new order for our relationships. It is more than loving our neighbors as ourselves. It is giving our enemies a giant and spontaneous bear hug. A bear hug that is bigger than *glasnost*. One that is not tied to Vietnamese policy in Cambodia. One that has nothing to do with their accounts of our MIAs. One that has nothing to do with the administration's goals in Washington or the self-preserving instincts of the leaders in Hanoi. But one that clearly demonstrates, for the entire world to see, the principle and power of reconciliation.

It's time to stand up. It's time to *walk around to the other side of the table*. It's time to see our neighbor and our friend and our enemy as God sees them—which is to say, as one and the same, indistinguishable one from the other. It's time to see the faces of all those who suffer the painful consequences of our continuing conflicts— interpersonal as well as international.

If reconciliation could happen in the hard places between the United States and Vietnam, it can happen anywhere in the world. It can happen between husband and wife across a bed. It can happen between neighbors across a backyard fence. If reconciliation could happen in Southeast Asia, the example might even set a creditable foundation for what could truly be a "new world order."

And each of us can and must work toward that, in whatever circumstances we find ourselves. For it is only through reconciled relationships that hurting human beings will ever find the peace so often missing in our world and in our own individual lives.

# Epilog

April 1991.

I must share one last image, a final Vietnamese face I encountered on the trip I took during the writing of the final pages of this manuscript.

* * * *

Twelve-year-old Hao sensed my frustration and put a calming hand on my arm. The two of us had begun putting a child's puzzle together, and I had just realized some of the pieces were missing.

Hao, a beautiful Vietnamese child with coal-black hair, warm brown eyes and an angelic face, adjusted to this problem much more easily than I did. Just as he has adjusted to so many things. Because he has had to.

Hao has polio. The gentle hand that calmed me was affixed to a pencil-thin arm. Hao can hardly weigh more than forty pounds. Both of his legs are afflicted, their use long gone. A set of small crutches are now Hao's constant companions.

I met Hao and we began work on the puzzle as he waited his turn on an exercise apparatus at the Thuy An Center—one of a hundred physically and/or mentally handicapped children who are institutionalized there about forty miles north of Hanoi.

Perhaps Hao could live outside the institution. But his father was crippled by the war and is now unable to work. There are three other children, all younger than Hao. The family finances are an ongoing act of desperation. Hao had to be removed from his family; there seemed no other choice. It isn't that his parents don't love him; his mother had come for a visit the morning I arrived. But cold, hard, practical reality dictates the terms of Hao's life.

So, like the puzzle he plays with, Hao's life is full of missing pieces. A brother and two sisters he rarely sees. Parents who are never there to tuck him in at night. Legs that no longer work. Even a complex picture puzzle that defies completion.

On my visit I saw that something else is now missing as well: the third meal of the day. The year's rice crop fell below expectations; fuel prices skyrocketed. Food is still available but only at greatly increased cost. Too costly for this segment of society. These are children—physically handicapped, some mentally retarded as well. They live on the margin of Vietnamese society, never allowed to expect much.

After meeting Hao I walked over to the center's kitchen where the second (and now last) meal of the day was about to be served. This was a special day; the children would have fish with their rice.

The lunchtime meal was like the child's puzzle—interesting some days, but never enough.

I looked around that room at the children. Beautiful children. Receptive, responsive, each having that certain gentleness that so often accompanies the realization of limitations—children waiting patiently for their lunch and for a world that has left them out on the margin of life. I saw symbol and reality all rolled into one.

I saw children struggling for wholeness against desperate odds. And I realized again how hard it is to find wholeness when some of the pieces are missing.

Or when there's a missing peace.

# Afterword

Ironically, at the very time I started actively working on this book about the missing peace in the Far East, Operation Desert Shield began in the Middle East. As I struggled to express my thoughts regarding the ongoing impact of my generation's war in Vietnam, Desert Shield became Desert Storm, and the war in the Persian Gulf became this generation's war. By the time I was working on the last chapters of this book and trying to articulate my thoughts on how we as individuals and a nation might finally put the Vietnam War behind us, our troops were returning from Saudi Arabia, Kuwait and Iraq to open-armed homecomings and ticker-tape parades.

So perhaps even more than most Vietnam veterans, I was forced to view the events in the Gulf through the filter of my own war experience in Vietnam. From the very beginning of the Gulf crisis and its initial massive military mobilization, I was struck by a recurring theme that seemed to drive both our military strategy and our diplomacy. "This will not be another Vietnam!"

As the opponents of American involvement in the Middle East looked for parallels, and as commentators, columnists and other political analysts compared and contrasted Vietnam and the Gulf, the clear determination of the U.S. administration and certainly of the military was: "This will not be another Vietnam!" Even those protesters who demonstrated against the buildup of forces, against the use of force, and eventually against the war itself were always quick to emphasize they weren't protesting against individual soldiers—only against the military action. Even as they tried to draw a philosophical parallel between Vietnam and the Gulf, they remembered the pain inflicted on Vietnam vets by war protesters and they wanted the focus to be different this time around. In that way the protesters too were saying, "This will not be another Vietnam!"

Yet, even as I noted the differences, a very personal family incident reminded me that in some ways all wars are the same.

Only days before the deadline President Bush had set for Iraq to withdraw from Kuwait, on the eve of what looked like almost certain war in the Gulf, my son Chris, a recent college grad, came home from his Marine Corps Officers' Training School to spend the 1990 Christmas holidays. With our entire family together, we had a wonderful and relaxing holiday.

And it was especially tough to take Chris to the airport at the end of his leave. As we said goodbye in the terminal, Margaret Ann began to cry. And I flashed back in my mind and my heart to the last time I'd seen my wife cry in an airport—standing in the rain on the tarmac in Moline, six months pregnant, waving goodbye to a Marine husband she couldn't be certain she would ever see again. Now here she was, twenty-three years later—the son she had borne now in the Marine uniform—saying a second painful goodbye to another young man preparing for war.

I could identify with Chris. I recalled the emotions I'd had when I'd been the one leaving: ready to do what I'd been trained to do; anxious to be a part of history; understanding for the first time the meaning of leaving home and separation from loved ones. But this time, as a father, as one staying behind, I had an additional and very different perspective. I suppose part of the difference was just time and age, but experience also makes a difference—I survived one war and have witnessed firsthand the impact of others. So *I prayed that my son wouldn't have to go.* And later I rejoiced that the war ended before he finished his final training.

Even as it took place, I realized our little family drama in that airport wasn't at all unique, our pain was no more than that experienced by hundreds of thousands of families with loved ones already in or heading for the Gulf. But for me it seemed like *déjà vu.* Seeing my wife crying in that airport, saying another wrenching goodbye, was an image that will never go away. It brought back all the emotions and issues written about in this book. And I knew that no matter what was said on a philosophical, military or diplomatic level, on the personal level you'd have had a hard time convincing Margaret Ann that the Persian Gulf War was very different from Vietnam.

Yet the contrasts and comparisons between the two wars continued to be made. And our national experience during and since the Gulf War certainly has significant implications for what has been said in this book. So I'd like to take a quick look at some of the possible connections.

I've heard some observers say that the only real similarity between the Gulf and Vietnam Wars was American involvement. While that may be a deliberate overstatement, certainly many differences are obvious. The difference in battlefield terrain—between open, barren desert and almost impenetrable jungle—was enormous. As a result, the style of combat was different; instead of the hand-to-hand guerrilla warfare of Vietnam jungles the Gulf War was won primarily with the technology of air power and other stand-off weaponry. Iraq proved to be a much less formidable enemy compared to North Vietnam. And because neither the Soviet Union nor China backed Saddam Hussein, there was no great worry that escalation might draw in another superpower.

Many of the differences resulted from deliberate decisions and planned policy. While "body count" had been an ongoing measure-ment of military effectiveness in Vietnam, that was not the case in the Gulf. The issue was dismissed in a single press-conference state-ment: "We will probably never know how many Iraqis died as a re-sult of Allied bombing."

And the American military obviously tried to correct what it felt were other serious mistakes in Vietnam, as evidenced by such tactics as the immediate massive deployment of forces, the setting of military strategy in the field rather than in Washington, and the careful control of media coverage. This time no one could say, "America isn't fighting to win," or, "The military had to fight with one hand behind its back." And this time, instead of underestimat-ing the enemy and promising a quick and easy victory, the military remained cautious and conservative and seemed to have overesti-mated the opposition's strength.

Perhaps because of some of these differences, the results too were different. The Gulf War ended more quickly than almost anyone could have hoped. Allied MIAs were few. The POWs came home within weeks. And American forces returned victorious to joyous homecomings sponsored by a country and a people determined not to spit on our soldiers this time but to treat them all as heroes.

Yet one big similarity is undeniable. As General Schwarzkopf acknowledged in his historic postwar press conference, the fact that our casualties were surprisingly light does nothing to lessen the tragedy for those who lost their loved ones.

That's true not just for the relatively few families of American casualties but also for the hundreds of thousands of Iraqi families who lost members in military and civilian deaths. As proven in Vietnam and yet again in the Gulf, war remains what it has been throughout history—a terrible, painful, inhuman means of settling differences between human beings.

As the months have passed since the end of the Gulf War, we

can begin to see in the Middle East what we've seen for years in the Far East—that *war does little to solve anything.* Once again we have proved that whenever human beings resort to armed conflict it is impossible to predict the outcome or the awful cost.

I regularly read *Indo-China Digest* to stay informed on what is happening in that part of the world. Even as the Persian Gulf War came to its "end," the ongoing events in Indo-China had changed little since the "end" of the Vietnam War. The fighting went on in Cambodia with resistance groups propped up by various and sundry forces, including the United States. Vietnam continued in economic chaos. And most of the basic issues we claim have separated us for a generation still remained.

We might have expected the Gulf situation to be different. After all, our military forces came home with a clear and overwhelming victory that destroyed all but a remnant of the enemy's offensive military power. Yet the Middle East in general and the Persian Gulf in particular remain a dangerous political, military, economic and diplomatic quagmire.

The best hopes we had for the region in the aftermath of the war have seriously unraveled. There's little or no democracy in Kuwait. And the Kuwaitis themselves, adopting an eye-for-an-eye philosophy of retribution, have been guilty of many of the same abuses inflicted on them by the Iraqis. While we sent Saddam Hussein and his forces running for home, he quickly turned his guns on his own people. So the poor Kurds in northern and western Iraq, like the Shiites in southern Iraq, suffer and will continue to suffer for pinning their hopes on the Allied coalition and opposing Saddam Hussein. On top of all this, we have no certainty that we've actually "defanged" Saddam of his nuclear poison. So despite any subsequent signs of hope in the Middle East—such as a growing willingness of Arabs and Israelis to sit down and talk—the Gulf War, like the one in Vietnam, settled little or nothing.

Then in the immediate aftermath of the war, so much was written about the possibility that the American experience in the Persian Gulf might finally, once and for all, put Vietnam behind us. That the speculation might indeed come true. That a clear, impressive military victory very well might "exorcise the ghost of Vietnam."

Though I would like to think optimistically, I don't believe any such exorcism took place. But then, I don't think an exorcism is really what we need.

While I'm sure the Gulf War forced a lot of Vietnam vets to face memories and emotions they might have suppressed for years, I suspect the speed with which the Gulf War ended allowed many of those vets to suppress those memories and emotions again before they really had time to deal with them in a healthy way. And my guess is that while Vietnam vets endorsed the wonderful welcome home the Gulf troops received—and some even marched in the parades and finally received applause themselves—the contrast with their own experience in the past had to open many old emotional wounds.

Lest we think America's amazing Gulf War victory can put the hurts and losses of Vietnam behind us forever, let me offer another caution. Our American military force was so impressive in the Persian Gulf that there's a danger of arrogance setting in. We could congratulate ourselves on having such incredible technological firepower that we will come to believe we can easily take care of any Third-World despot with the same ease. And if we begin to base our foreign policy on that kind of thinking we may soon find ourselves in a situation where another war like Vietnam is inevitable.

Or we could feel so proud of our military successes in liberating Kuwait that we will adopt the Persian Gulf War as "the war of our generation" and forget all about Vietnam, in the same way our parents' generation views World War 2 as "their war" and almost discounts the Korean War. But if we do that, if we let the success in the Gulf push Vietnam off the stage of our national consciousness forever, we may never recover. And the welcome sound of our long-sought victory celebrations could permanently drown out the cries of ongoing human suffering in Southeast Asia.

On a more hopeful note, the implications of our Persian Gulf experience could bode well for America and Vietnam. Perhaps the taste of victory we experienced in routing the forces of Saddam Hussein will enable us to feel strong enough and proud enough again as a nation to be gracious winners. If so, maybe that strength and pride and graciousness can carry over into our relationship with Vietnam.

Throughout the Gulf crisis, the Allied coalition and the unprecedented cooperation of the greatest superpowers on earth prompted a lot of talk about what was called "a new world order." While such international cooperation was indeed a wonderful and hopeful relief from the cold-war model of conflict and discord we've known for forty-plus years, I think we could do better than to look to the Gulf War, or any war for that matter, as the blueprint of a new world order. Indeed, a more impressive model might yet develop out of Southeast Asia. In recent months there are more positive signs. In the spring of 1991 the U.S. government granted its first postwar aid to Vietnam, a million dollars of which was channeled to Vietnam through World Vision and its programs. In October 1991 Secretary of State James Baker announced the easing of travel restrictions to allow more Americans to visit Vietnam and the opening of negotiations to normalize diplomatic relations with Hanoi.

Many roadblocks to reconciliation remain. But the deep and lasting wounds of Vietnam will never be healed until we understand it is never a sign of weakness to reach out in reconciliation—even in an attempt to help the person who bloodied our nose. From a biblical, theological and moral point of view it would be an act of strength. Indeed, true reconciliation in Vietnam and elsewhere is the missing piece in a solid foundation on which to build not just a new world order but a *better* world.